Diving in the Maldives

HUVADHOO

the forgotten atoll

Alexander von Mende

Brambleby Books

Diving in the Maldives – Huvadhoo, the forgotten atoll
© Alexander von Mende 2011

All Rights Reserved

No part of this book may be reproduced in any form
by photocopying or by any electronic or mechanical means,
including information, storage or retrieval systems,
without permission in writing from both the copyright
owner and the publisher of this book.

Alexander von Mende has asserted his right under the Copyright, Design and Patent
Act, 1988, to be identified as author of this work.

ISBN 9781908241030

Cover design and book layout by Vincent Gaufreteau
Illustrations and artwork by Tibeon

Published by Brambleby Books Ltd.
www.bramblebybooks.co.uk

Printed and bound by Cambrian Printers, Aberystwyth, UK, using FSC paper.

*In memory of my father,
Georgios Dimitriou,
who introduced me to diving and the fascinating world of marine life.*

16 July 1961 - 27 September 2008

Contents

Introduction 7

Chapter 1 — The Maldives 9
    History 10
    Geology 14
    Huvadhoo – the forgotten atoll 16

Chapter 2 — Diving Huvadhoo 21
    Types of dive sites 22
    Dive sites 24
        Partial solar eclipse 27
        My very first dive in the Maldives ... 32
        Dives with Chris 37
        Dives with Michael 41
        Dives with JP 56

Chapter 3 — Identification guide 61
    Groups index 63
        Reef symbioses 64
        Coral reef ecology and conservation ... 82
        Shark biology 106
        Ecological dive etiquette 198

Index 201
    Dive sites by type 202
    Icons 204
    Common and scientific names 207

About the author 219
Acknowledgements 220
Photographic references 220

Deen at Nilandhoo Kandu

Introduction

Huvadhoo. The sound of the name alone seems to evoke pure magic. It literally evaporates and obscures the senses. Pictures of palm trees that bend over the sea in the rising heat, the rushing of silent waves over virgin white sand and everything glimmers in memories. Just long enough that is, until a cool wave sweeps around your bare feet.

Yes, this atoll is like a mirage but its attractions are of terrestrial origin. Their seduction is absolutely real, yet successfully continues to resist a proper explanation. This last forgotten atoll of the Maldives awakes the longings of our childhood for adventure and discovery. It will not let you down. Even though it just lies there: vast, proud and calm, right in the middle of the mighty Indian Ocean, silently whispering of its treasures. There are many hidden here, but none is retrieved easily.

Just as with all great fortunes, it takes a certain kind of patience and manner of searching to acquire them; some are of a spiritual and some of a physical nature. Maldivians are proud and yet very laid back at the same time. Their rich culture lies openly in their islands but demands a persuasive form of patience to make them tell you its secrets. Unfortunately, many of their stories have been lost already and you have to dig deep if you insist on finding them. Yet the unseen is still a vivid part of their daily lives, as it helps in questions of love, money and social justice. Even so, Maldivians like to hide this fact from western eyes and ears, presumably thinking they could be perceived as superstitious.

For other treasures you simply have to look up. You will quickly discover them. After all it was the sun that made all this Maldivian beauty grow. A lot melts in the play of its blinding light and the swaying shadows of palm trees. Other things appear as clean and lucid as you have ever seen in your life. While during the night there comes a moment when you ask yourself if you are actually still on the same planet. The stars shine so much brighter and stronger. Their small brothers and sisters can still be seen here, where there is nothing around but ocean; deep, silent, dark ocean. Now it is right here where the mightiest treasure of Huvadhoo is concealed: the deepest and least explored coral reefs of all the islands in the Maldives.

Chapter 1

The Maldives

Chapter 1 — The Maldives

History

Early times

The political history of the Maldives began, like many other islands of this region, most likely with the colonisation by Indian fishermen in the 5th century BC. Around 1,600 years later, in the year 1153, the Maldivians were proselytised to Islam by the Arabian traveller Abu al Barakat. This event also marks the beginning of official historiography and the introduction of the sultanate. It is still celebrated today as 'The day Maldives embraced Islam'. Up to this time, the islands were a Buddhist kingdom. However, it appears that the official change of religion did not have much of an effect on the common folk. When, approximately 200 years later, the Moroccan Marco Polo, Ibn Battuta, visited the islands, he could not report anything friendly about Maldivian women and their revealing dress code, which was basically a bare chest! His success as a local judge was arguable, as his strict orthodox Muslim judgements were simply ignored. After nine months he had lost his initial credibility with the locals and left the atolls. The Buddhistic roots of Maldivian culture can still be felt today in their moderate interpretation of Islam.

Colonisation attempts

The next historically important events were a series of colonisation attempts by European countries. The first was led by the Portuguese who established a trading post in 1558. Fifteen years later, they were driven out by Muhammad Thakurufaanu Al-Azam and his brother, after the Portuguese tried to convert them to the Christian faith. The brothers became heroes and their deeds gave rise to the National Day.

The next colonisation attempt came from the Dutch, who had just wrested power over the Indian Ocean from the Portuguese, during the 17th century. They claimed hegemony over the Maldives but did not interfere directly in internal affairs. In 1796, they were chased away by the British Royal Navy who put the atolls under their protection. It was only in 1887 that this protectorate became officially signed by both parties. As with the Dutch, the British did not get involved in internal affairs and only voiced their claims in military and foreign affairs. The protectorate continued, with some minor interruptions, until Maldivian independence was declared in 1965.

Until 1932 the power of the chief minister increased to the point that a constitutional monarchy was introduced. In 1953, the Maldives proclaimed a very short-lived republic under their first president, Mohammad Amin Didi. Unfortunately, some of his reforms, including women's rights, were regarded as too modern for some of his more conservative Muslim compatriots who consequently subverted his rule. He was beaten to death in 1954 in a revolt against food shortages. After this brief excursion into the realms of democracy, the sultanate resumed their rule until 1968. In between, some of the darkest and most bitter events in the history of the Huvadhoo atoll occurred.

United Suvadive Republic

In 1959, the Addu Atoll announced their independence from the central government in Malé and proclaimed the United Suvadive Republic. The apparent reason for this was a lack of vitally important products for daily life and likely encouragement by the British that maintained an airfield on their islands. In the run-up to this event the central government had declared new taxes, as well as passport and visa regulations in order to undermine the independent and profitable trade of the southern islands with Ceylon and India. Huvadhoo and Famulhaa quickly joined the Addu Atoll.

As a first reaction, the government in Malé sent a gunboat under the direct command of Prime Minister Ibrahim Nasir to the Atoll of Huvadhoo. He threatened island chiefs and other personalities of the region and thereby halted Huvadhoo's support to the republic. The other two atolls were spared, which caused the separatist movement to continue.

In the meantime, Prime Minister Nasir's efforts to convince the British to stop their already vague support for the separatists finally yielded success. The Suvadivian ships that had been sent to India and Ceylon were captured and not allowed to leave harbour. This caused another lack of vital products in Huvadhoo and made them rejoin the Suvadivian movement in their so called 'Second Revolt'. What followed was the darkest chapter in Maldivian history.

On the 2nd February 1962, a ship arrived in today's Tinadhoo. It was sent by the government in Malé and several hundred soldiers and militia volunteers disembarked. They destroyed the entire infrastructure of the island, while the inhabitants had to wait and watch in shoulder deep water. They took some 200 to 300 prisoners, whose whereabouts are still unknown. The rest of the population was forced to leave the island. The ship continued to Famulhaa, where it tried to dock, but was stopped by the people. Ultimately, the expedition and eviction caused more than 2,400 dead according to unofficial estimates and set the scene for the capitulation of the United Suvadive Republic in 1963. Tinadhoo was resettled only three years later. The event was only officially commemorated for the first time in 2009.

Modern Times

After independence in 1965, the constitutional Sultanate reverted back to a republic for the second time in 1968. Ibrahim Nasir became its first president. During the 1970s the important fish trade with Sri Lanka collapsed, while the British abandoned their military base in 1976. By 1978, triggered by an economic crisis and a steep decline in popularity, Nasir was forced to flee to Singapore.

He was succeeded by Maumoon Abdul Gayoom, who would govern the country for 30 years. His policy to develop the poorest islands first made him very popular. The first tourist resort had already opened in 1972, but it was during his reign that the Maldives developed into the dream destination that they are today.

In October 2008, Mohamed Nasheed was elected president. In the meantime more than 100 resorts were built, offering some 20,000 beds. In addition, Maldivians operate over 150 live-aboard diving vessels that offer accommodation for another 2,000 guests. In 2008, almost 700,000 people visited the Maldives and spent 5.5 million nights there! The tourism industry makes up in access of 30% of the country's income. A truly remarkable achievement.

In Huvadhoo there are only three resorts – Jumeirah, Alila and Robinson. However, it is planned that this number will increase to six within the next few years. This means divers who like to dive alone or in small groups, rather than sharing a dive site with several boats, would be wise to travel pretty soon.

Ibrahim Nasir — Republic of Maldives first president

Geology

The existence of the Maldives is intrinsically tied to its geological and biological past; it would simply not exist without these two governing processes.

From a geographical perspective the Maldives are resting on a 2000km long submarine ridge that connects the Laccadives, Maldives and the islands of Chagos, from north to south. The ridge itself is most likely of volcanic origin, while the Maldivian aragonite basement developed by the end of the last ice age, around 15,000 years ago. The melting land-based ice caused the sea level to rise by more than 100m. Instead of drowning, the corals just grew in pursuit of the light and thereby formed the Maldives. Accordingly, the biogenic aragonite basement must also be at least 100m thick.

Aragonite skeleton formation by corals is responsible for creating the base of the Maldives in more ways than one. The enormous speed of crystallisation in hermatypic corals is due thanks to the extremely successful symbiosis between animal coral polyps and plant protozoans. The tiny algae live in the thin skin of the polyps and produce vast amounts of sugar by means of photosynthesis. This energy source enables hermatypic stony corals to build up their skeletons by orders of magnitudes faster than ahermatypic corals, corals without such symbiotic algae.

With regard to recently predicted rises of the sea level, the people of the Maldives are well aware. Unfortunately, rising sea levels are only part of the problem, because most people tend to forget two other factors that come along with climate change – acidification of the seas and increased rates of coral bleaching. Both factors negatively influence coral growth. While increased atmospheric CO_2-levels acidify the oceans and thereby only slow the process of calcification, coral bleaching usually results in high coral mortality and therefore entirely halts the reef building process. However, these factors are relative if the speeds at which corals must have grown during the end of the last ice age are examined. At that time, sea levels rose up to 1.5m in 100 years, which is a lot faster than the predicted 60cm until 2100. A final judgement on whether the Maldives will drown like Atlantis is therefore a very difficult one to make.

Huvadhoo – the forgotten atoll

Location

The Maldives are located in the centre of the northern Indian Ocean, south-west of the tip of the Indian subcontinent. They stretch over a distance of almost 800km. Between the far northern Ihavandhippolhoo, the district of Haa Atoll, and the southern Addu, are about 1,200 islands stringing along as an apparently near endless necklace of pearls. The atolls are parallel to one another in the middle part, while they fuse into large rings in the north and south.

Huvadhoo in the south stands out as being the widest of them all. The southern tip of Huvadhoo is just 10km north of the equator. Further south are the tiny island of Fomulhaa and the small Addu Atoll. Huvadhoo is divided into two districts, Ghaaf Alif in the north and Ghaaf Dhaal in the south. It is one of the largest atolls in the world, covering an area almost 70km wide, more than 80km long and comprising 235 islands, of which 20 are inhabitedf. The human population is approximately 30,000. The recently opened resort islands, Meradhoo, Funamaudoo and Hadahaa, are located in a central axis from the east to the west of the atoll. This explains why the dive sites presented in this book are mainly found in the central parts of the western and eastern ring, as well as in the centre of the atoll. Furthermore, the atoll is about 70m deep on average, which complicates an effective search for good and adequate dive sites for recreational divers. For these reasons, it will take a while until the entire atoll is properly fathomed. Join in!

Chapter 1 — The Maldives

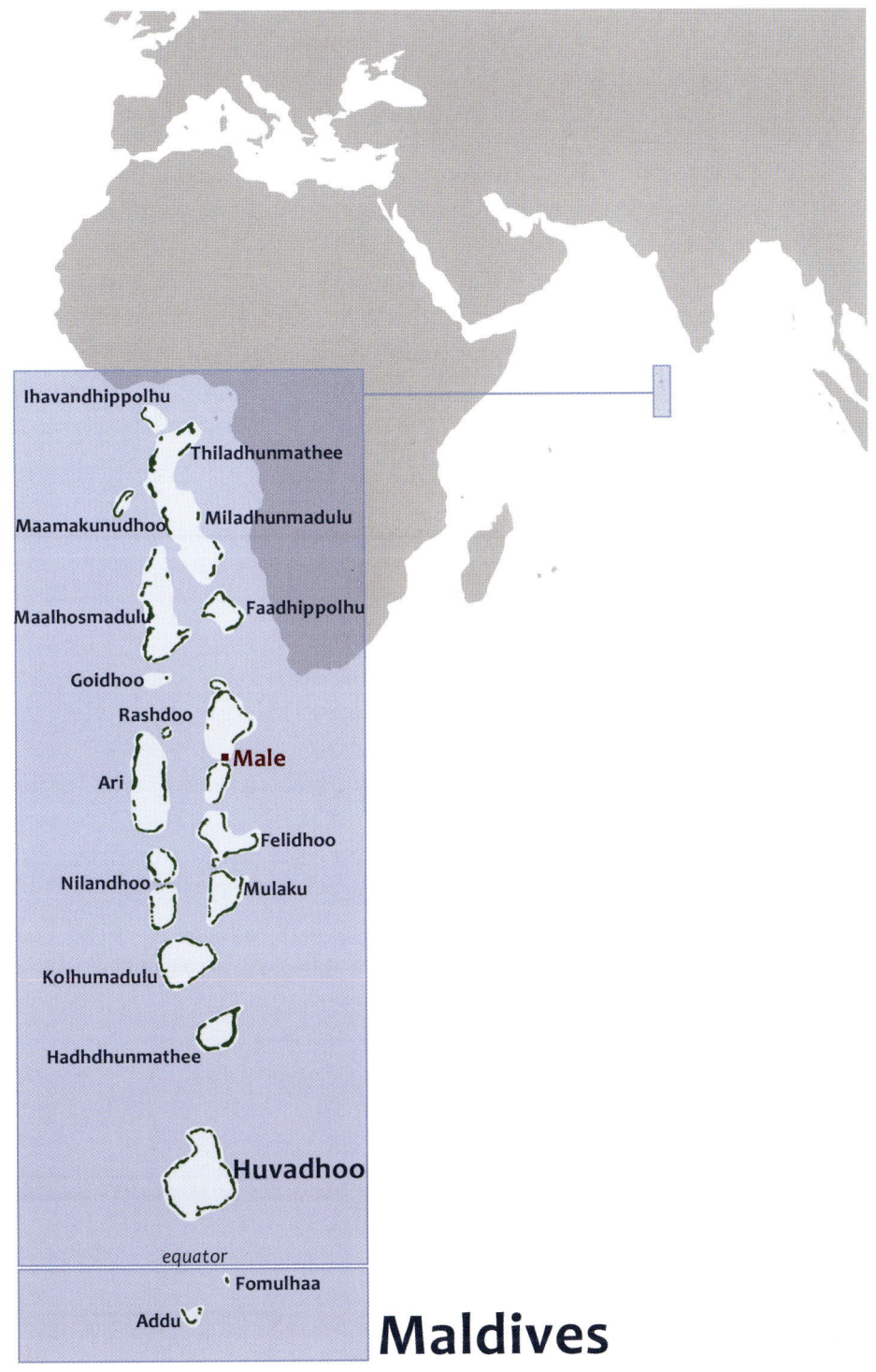

Maldives

Climate and weather

As might be expected from a place so near the equator, it is hot and humid throughout the year. Temperatures range on average between a 'cold' 26°C to an agreeable 30°C and do not fall much below 25°C during the night. Water temperatures fall into line with values around 28°C that do not change much until 30m.

The monsoon winds control the local climate regime. Between December and April the air above India cools down, while it heats up over Africa. The resulting circulation of sinking cold and rising hot air pulls a constant north-eastern wind over the north-west Indian Ocean. As cold air cannot store much water, especially when it is blown over dry land, this is comparatively dry for the Maldives. Statistically, only four days of refreshing rain occur during January and February, making this period the most popular travel time, high season in fact.

While the sun's zenith approaches the Tropic of Cancer at the beginning of April, the monsoon shifts its direction to south-west by mid-May at the latest. The circulation starts turning in exactly the opposite sense. On its way from Africa over the open ocean, the air heats up and accumulates loads of heavy rain-laden clouds. They rid themselves of their heavy burden in short but intense showers. Don't be afraid though, the largest part remains in the clouds and doesn't fall until it reaches India. There the streets will be inundated, and the people celebrate the end of the dry season. For the Maldives this season has an average of 12 days of rain per month. Therefore, the sun is still shining during more than half of the days.

Currents and tides

The monsoon is also the driving force behind the water currents, with a slight delay just as the wind shifts its direction twice during the year. During the north-east monsoon, the ocean pushes against the eastern side of the atoll and vice versa during the south-west monsoon. This is of immense importance for channel dives because channels are usually dived during the incoming tide. Hence the tidal current is either strengthened or weakened, according to the prevailing monsoon. Since the strength of the current constitutes the relevant criterion for the presence of large fish, it is often the monsoon that dictates the quality of a dive site. For the Huvadhoo atoll this means that diving is better on the east side during the north-east monsoon and the west side during the south-east monsoon. In this respect, Huvadhoo has the major advantage that no surrounding atoll weakens the strength of the monsoon during either season.

Chapter 2

Diving Huvadhoo

Types of dive sites

When you dive in the Maldives, you will invariably encounter a number of typically Maldivian diving-related names and expressions. The word 'reef' is simply not sufficient to reflect the local diversity of the world below. The following list provides a short introduction in order to try and help you improve communication between you and your local dive guide.

House reefs

This is not actually a special type of reef as such but more likely the first reef you will see during your holidays. It is in fact the reef that surrounds your island, the arena of mandatory check dives and the playground of experienced divers that like to dive without a professional guide. Very often it is also much cheaper to dive here because boat fees can be saved. Some people spend their entire holidays diving on the house reef only, as this is often quite large and combines different aspects of the various types of coral reefs generally encountered.

Farus

Farus are reefs that surround islands on the inside of the atoll. Therefore your island's house reef is a faro. These reefs are usually very easy to dive on. It is unlikely that a faru will ever be among the most beautiful dive sites you will encounter but they do usually offer very satisfying dives. The distance of the island to the atoll ring is a good general indication of how much fish life you can expect. The closer the better. Dhevvamaagelaa is a great example, as it seemingly always manages to surprise divers with something unexpected.

Giris

Giris are very shallow underwater pinnacles. These reefs reach just under the water surface. During extreme low tides, single coral heads can sometimes even be seen protruding above the water. Maldivians use to define a giri as a place that you cannot pass over in a boat. They usually comprise very nice dive sites. The closer to the surrounding ocean and more isolated they are, the better. Dhevva Giri in central Huvadhoo is a great dive site.

Thilas

Thilas are the deeper counterparts to giris. They are defined as reefs that you can pass over in a boat at any time. Such reefs are a Maldivian speciality and some of them unquestionably belong to the most stunning dive sites of the world. Just as with giris, they become better the closer they are to the atoll ring and the more isolated they are from other reefs. There are many beautiful thilas in Huvadhoo but Mas and Hafsa Thila in the west are, in my experience, the best. It is a reasonable expectation that other thilas will be discovered in Huvadhoo in the future.

Fushis

These reefs are located on the outside of the atoll facing the ocean. They resemble farus but are exposed to much stronger currents due to their location. There is only one good known dive site of this type in Huvadhoo – Maafushi Beyru.

Kandus

Kandus are probably the reason why the Maldives became so famous among divers. In Dhivehi, the Maldivian language, 'kandu' actually means the open ocean. Don't worry though, when your divemaster refers to a kandu he does not mean the wide open blue water beyond the reef, but rather the channels that connect the open ocean with the sea within the atoll. At these dive sites the presence of large groups of sharks is almost guaranteed, especially during strong incoming tides. Nilandhoo Kandu in the east is a truly stunning dive site and can easily be regarded as one of the best channel dives in the Maldives. Drift experience is absolutely essential when tackling such reefs.

Chapter 2 — Diving Huvadhoo

Dive sites

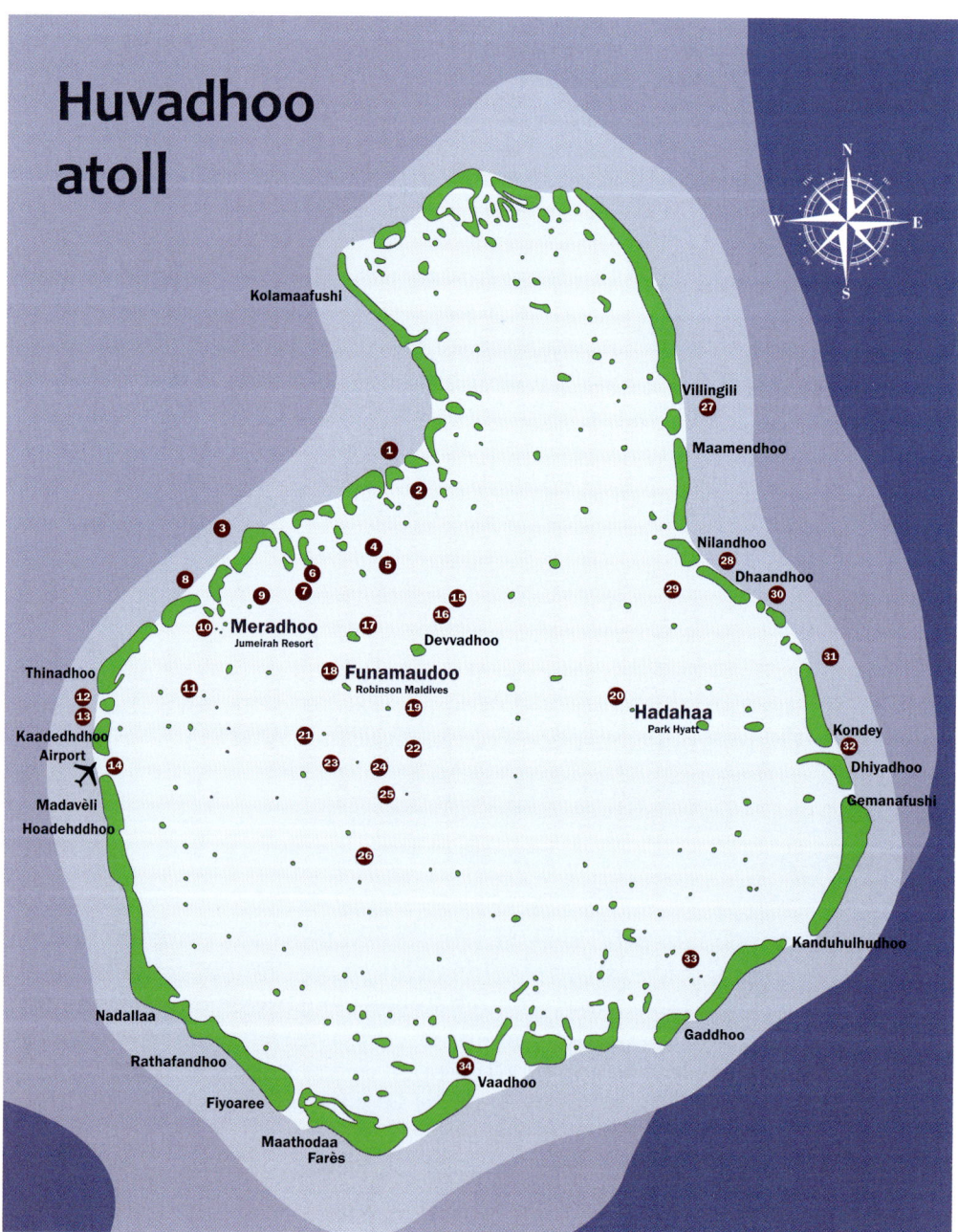

Dive sites index

West
1 – Fulangi Kandu	26
2 – Fulangi Thila	27
3 – Maafushi Beyru	29
4 – Mas Thila	30
5 – Wagaathu Gala	31
6 – Coral City	34
7 – Hafsa Thila	35
8 – Meradhoo Kandu	36
9 – Meradhoo Thila	36
10 – Cabbage Thila	38
11 – Haodi Galaa Giri	38
12 – Kafena Kandu	39
13 – Rahadhoo Kandu	40
14 – Kaadedhdhoo Kandu	40

Central
15 – Dheeva Thila	42
16 – Dheeva Giri	43
17 – Dhevvamaagalaa Faru	44
18 – Funamaudoo Faru, Club Robinson Maldives	46
19 – Hagedhoo Faru	47
20 – Hirifushi Faru	48
21 – Gosi Faru	48
22 – Leon's Giri	49
23 – Baulhageella Faru	50
24 – Kuda Giri	50
25 – Bodu Giri	51
26 – Beyru Ha Thila	52

East
27 – Villingili Kandu	53
28 – Nilandhoo Kandu	54
29 – Nilandhoo Thila	52
30 – Vodamulaa Kandu	55
31 – Marehaa Kandu	58
32 – Kondey Kandu	58
33 – Mafzoo Giri	59
34 – Vadhoo Thila	59

1 – Fulangi Kandu

Fulangi is Dhivehi for 'flying fish' and this name is quite accurately chosen because it is very likely that you will see some of these flighty fish on your way to the channel when they are fleeing from the bow of the boat. The dive usually begins on the north-east side of the outer reef. Here you quickly drop down to 30m because of the strong current. Between the outer reef and a small offshore thila you make your way towards the corner of the channel. It is advisable to take a short break at the corner itself, in order to spot some sharks. Don't worry in case you don't find any here, as there is a second chance towards the end of the dive. You will continue inside the channel along its eastern side that is flanked by another parallel thila. Towards its end, chances arise to again meet up with these elegant predators. On the way there you should regularly look at the bottom of the channel, where sharks often take a nap on the sand.

N 00.41.750, E 073.12.850
Depth: 5-30m
Fish: ★★★★★
Corals: ★★★★★
Current: 2-4 (5)
Speciality: Strong current and thus lots of fish

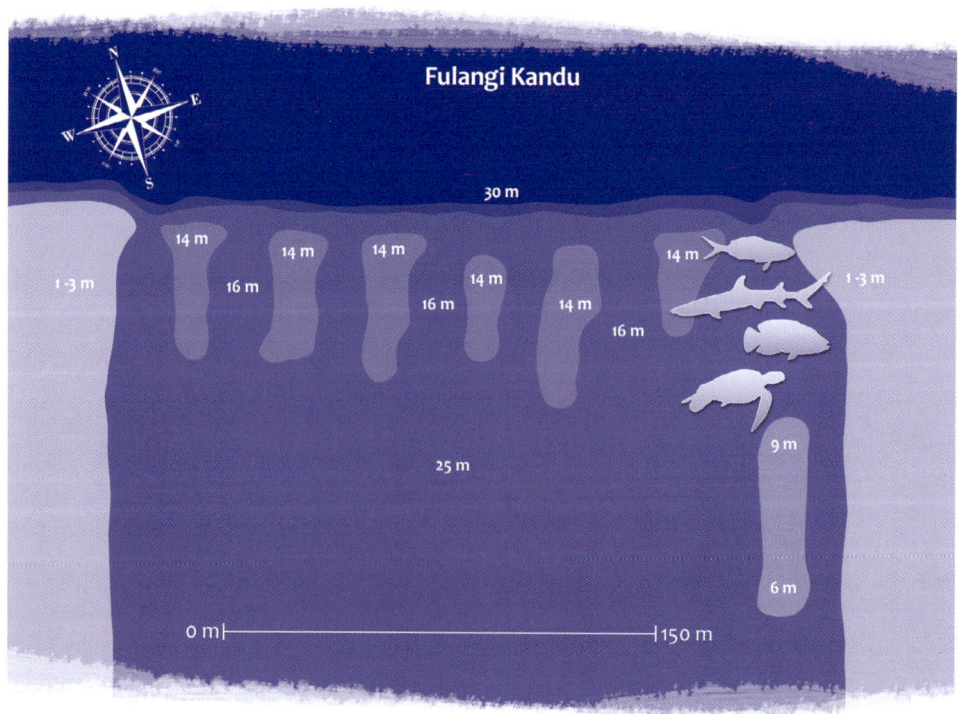

2 – Fulangi Thila

This thila is actually not one single massive coral structure but a number of smaller pillars located further inside the Fulangi channel. The individual pillars feature tightly packed table corals and other *Acropora* species. These are separated by sandy patches on the ground, which makes it possible for divers to observe both sandy bottom and coral associated species. Divers should always keep a look out for the shy Leopard Sharks dozing on the sandy patches. Eagle rays have also been observed here, flying above the heads of divers.

The thila is best dived during incoming tides and hence approached from the north. The stronger the current the more fish, especially sharks, are usually found.

N 00.41.000, E 073.14.000
Depth: 8 - 30m
Fish: ★★★☆☆
Corals: ★★★★☆
Current: 2-4(5)
Speciality: White-tip Reef and Leopard Sharks

Partial solar eclipse

The weather is gentle and the sea lies calmly ahead of us. A perfect day for a little joyride to the outer reef to spot some dolphins. At first it's a bit choppy and the boat surges forward in mighty jumps, leaving nothing but a crystal blue track of agitated water in its wake. We turn around the next inhabited island, to take a glimpse at the natives, but they are hiding from the sun and the heat unaware how soon they will seek warmth today. Never mind, we wanted to see dolphins anyway. So the speedboat lunges again over the waves, half flying, half sliding. At full speed towards the outer ring. I am standing at the front of the boat, wind coursing through my hair, heart pumping heavily in anticipation. Eyes on the horizon. Where are they?

When we pass the first islands, the sea becomes more calm. We are entering the Indian Ocean. Vast and powerful, it whispers that it has no end. The waves seem small, until we realise that they are actually hills made of water. Hundreds of metres wide, they lift the boat gently up and down. You do not want to believe your eyes in view of their size, but they force you to; they are folding the horizon. They make you understand that there is something beyond your understanding and even your imagination. Their sheer presence makes me shiver in awe. They don't care.

For a moment, a cloud covers the sun and turns the water slightly darker. Something is different it seems, something strange, just a second before we spot the Brown Noddies. The native fishermen use them to find tuna fish, but for us they show the way to the dolphins. The first flock yields nothing, nor the second, and we are already far outside. The lifting hills of the ocean only help a little. We are cruising, eyes wide open and scanning the horizon. Then once again this strange feeling arises that there is something else in our way, something bigger, something immensely powerful. The light, I think…

"THERE!", the captain shouts, stretching his left arm westward. He must have seen something. His face has changed too. It's excited and concentrated as he powers the boat towards our new direction. Then we see them, one, two, maybe even three dolphins ripping through the surface. They come closer and my eyes open wide. It's not three of them, more likely ten or twenty. They are all around our boat, jumping in curiosity. We motor on and they position themselves right in front of our bow. No matter how fast we go they keep up, some even jump ahead. They have no fear, it seems. Full of joy, they play and look at us as they jump next to the boat. I hold my hand out over the water, hoping they might like to brush against it, but suddenly they all veer north and south, leaving us alone again. I wonder in a state of bewilderment, are they afraid of my hand?

The hand looks different, actually around us everything looks different. Where have all the colours gone, why does everything suddenly seem so quiet? Am I alone? We exchange a glance. No, they also see it. In these moments, time can flow like cold honey. Even the waves seem to duck their heads in eerie anticipation. What has changed? Our looks fly in all directions, but there is only horizon around us and it becomes ever darker. Has yet another cloud covered the sun? We look up and there it is. Something more mighty has darkened the sun. Now we can see it, from behind the cloud a mere sickle shines in agony. The moon has stolen most of the sun's power. Goose bumps and shivers creep over my skin. What a sight.

As we arrive back at the resort, the sand reveals its true colour; it is just as yellow as any other sand in the whole wide world, only the sun here makes it look bride white.

3 – Maafushi Beyru

Maafushi Beyru is a classical dive site on the outer atoll ring. The reef resembles a modern dyke that gently slopes downwards and thereby creates an enormous coral garden. This is intersected by several trenches that follow the coastline. They are filled with sand and harbour many sand-dwelling species such as flounders and Garden Eels. Together with the coral-associated species the spot displays great biodiversity. The speciality of the site is a huge resident Napoleon fish. Due to the exposed location, the current is usually quite strong; therefore diving at Maafushi Beyru requires some drift experience.

N 00.39.981, E 073.12.810
Depth: 5-30m
Fish: ★★★★★
Corals: ★★★★★
Current: 2-4
Speciality: a huge resident Napoleon fish

4 – Mas Thila

Mas Thila is a real jewel in the western region of the Huvadhoo atoll. The name means 'many fish' and it definitely deserves it. Basically, the thila is a prolongation of Wagaathu Gala, a little further south-east. The difference between these two spots is the increased likeliness of shark sightings at Mas Thila, which can be explained by stronger currents. The two diving sites are divided by a small valley that features a beautiful coral garden. Here you can find otherwise rarely seen colourful varieties of soft corals. The middle part of the thila is the most beautiful and hence you start the dive, depending on the direction of the current, either slightly behind the north-western end, or at the valley in the south-east. The current strength can vary a lot between moderate to strong but will always carry you comfortably along the reef. Mas Thila usually offers a classic drift dive and provides a constant stream of impressions, just like being in the cinema. Certainly one of the best dive sites in Huvadhoo.

N 00.38.200, E 073.11.425
Depth: 5-30m
Fish: ★★★★☆
Corals: ★★★☆☆
Current: 1-2
Speciality: Sharks

Dive sites | Chapter 2 — Diving Huvadhoo

5 – Wagaathu Gala

Wagaathu Gala in Dhivehi means 'Sand bank of thieves'. The story tells of fishermen who stole equipment from their rivals' boats. They hid it under the corals of the galaa in order to eventually recover it for later use. Whether the story is actually true or not is of little concern as it gives us a far better piece of advise, namely to look under coral blocks. Extremely rare sights in Huvadhoo have been seen here, such as Giant Leaf Fish and Stone Fish. This place will captivate you in other ways too, with its wealth of opulent coral gardens and enormous fish swarms. You can also meet gigantic Napoleons and the elegantly flying eagle rays.

Just as at Mas Thila, the current dictates the starting point and it makes no real difference as both directions are absolutely worthwhile. You can either start from the ditch between the two, or slightly north-west from the sand bank. For sure, you won't miss the ditch where thousands of fish cross from one side of the elongated thila to the other. Basically you only have to put yourself right in the middle of this street crossing and enjoy the show. The current is usually a bit weaker than at Mas Thila and thus the perfect alternative if it gets too wild there. It is one of the favourite dive sites of the author.

N 00.37.650, E 073.11.700
Depth: 5-30m
Fish: ★★★★★
Corals: ★★★★★
Current: 2-3
Speciality: Endless coral gardens and fish swarms

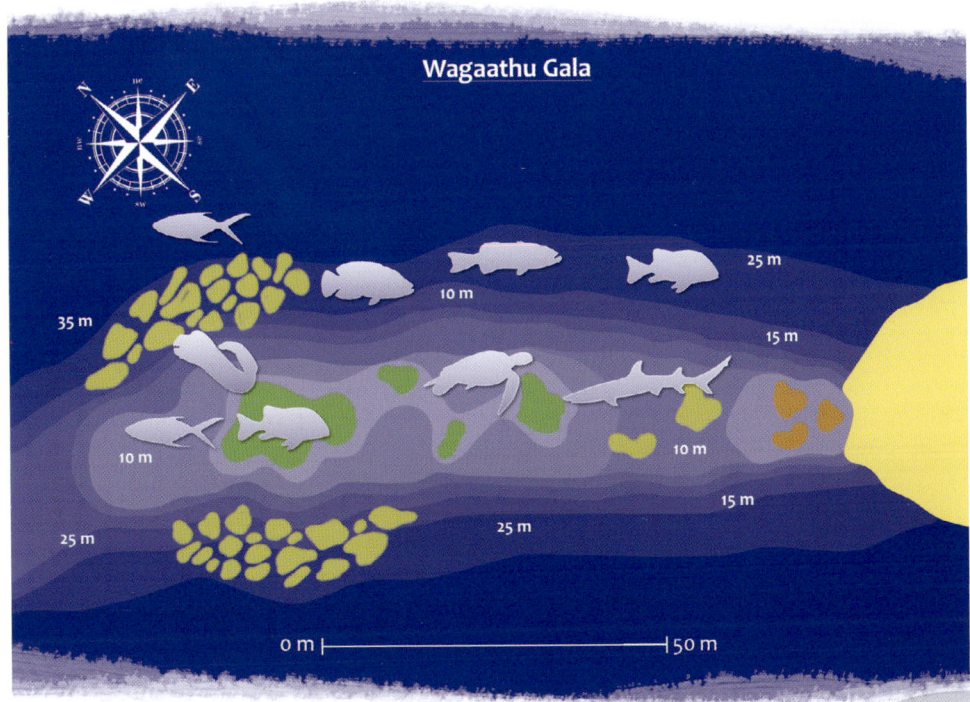

My very first dive in the Maldives

It was pretty early in the morning when we directed our provisional diving-dhoni to Mas Thila for my very first dive in Huvadhoo. There were still no guests on the island, as the resort had not opened yet and would not for another two weeks. There were only four of us in the boat, Chris and Lena, diving instructors, our divemaster Deen and I, the biologist. I was additionally excited as this would be my first dive on a coral reef, the last major marine habitat that I had yet to see. Diving the rainforest of the seas is the ultimate experience for any marine ecologist.

The long boat ride calmed my excitement, but not for long. Despite the fact the equatorial sun was burning down on my pale skin, I could not stay in the shadow of the bridge but had to sit on the tip of the bow. There were flying fish in front of us, hastily jumping away from the boat. The sea lay calm and in it a multitude of forgotten palm islands, just as Daniel Defoe had described them. All my life I had dreamt of seeing this environment and now, as the dream finally became true, I was too overwhelmed to actually realise what was happening, even though the best was still ahead of me.

Obviously I was nervous like a little boy facing his first day at school when we finally reached Mas Thila. I was so exhausted from the past events, just minutes ago, that I almost slipped when I jumped into the crystal clear water, but once the familiar silence embraced my heavily beating heart, the feeling of security returned immediately and the air ran freely into my lungs. Hundreds and thousands of yellow striped, blue fusiliers were among the first fish I spotted. There must have been a hidden, inexhaustible source of them, somewhere in the reef, or maybe back there just around the corner. They circled us, or so it seemed, as they were everywhere. When they had passed, I could finally see the corals for the first time in my life, the builders of biodiversity and natural opulence. However, the colours where surprisingly dull – all kinds of green and brown but none of the bright gleaming tints we all know from the magazines. How could that be?

The answer came quickly: the presence of soft corals was in fact near zero. Huvadhoo is not a paradise of colourful soft corals but of their stony counterpart that inspire by mind: twisting shapes rather than colours. Their abundance and diversity is staggering. I spotted all sorts of Acropora species, from gigantic table corals that easily span over 2m wide as well as fragile Staghorns with hundreds of branches. They stood right next to brain corals and massive *Porites* species, sprinkled with flashy Christmas Tree Worms. I was truly stunned as I drifted motionless with the current.

Incapable of taking my eyes off all this beauty I missed my first sharks. Though, even if I would have looked up and around me, which I did a little later, I only saw my dive buddies wildly waving their flat hand about their face and pointing into the blue. It looked as if they'd defend themselves from a two finger eye-strike of an imaginary karate kid, whom they took revenge on by poking their index finger into the opponent's throat. Later, on the boat, I learnt the meaning of this wild gesturing but for now we were still down under, where my irritated expression drove my buddies to despair. At this point the sharks had passed and my friends gave up on me.

For the following part of the reef we had split up into parties of two. I joined our assistant base leader, Chris, who had already seen many Maldivian reefs. The beauty of Mas Thila also enraptured him as he took loads of pictures and made one video after the other with his digital camera – a toy that I would fall in love with very soon after. Nevertheless, he passed by the first turtle that I saw and which took a rest in-between two coral heads. For a magic moment we glanced at one another. The turtle showed no signs of fear whatsoever. Unfortunately, I had to get after my buddy, as he was way ahead of me. It should not be the last turtle I would see during my time at this diving site.

Eventually, I ran out of air and so the dive came to its natural end. Back on the boat, everybody talked about the great sharks they had seen, that they had never expected so many of them, whether I had seen them too and what I thought about them. I replied that I had not seen any. They insisted that they had pointed them out to me... and then I learned about the meaning of the karate kid.

6 – Coral City

Coral City deserves its name just as much as the Garden of Eden does its. The coral heads stretch seemingly endlessly along the reef. It is difficult to find a single spot that is not covered but shows sand instead. Biology enthusiasts will have a great time observing the Darwinian notion of the 'Survival of the fittest'; in this case the competition for space and sunlight. For this reason and because of the often weak current, many different kinds of *Acropora* table corals dominate the site. Some of them reach 3m across. Fish life is almost absent except of some smaller swarms of fusiliers every now and then. Apart from these you will find mainly reef top-associated species like Butterfly Fish and Surgeons. This dive site is not suited for divers looking for fish, but a pure delight for people in love with stony corals. It is best dived during an incoming current.

N 00.37.860, E 73.09.290
Depth: 5-20m
Fish: ★★ ★ ★ ★
Corals: ★ ★ ★ ★ ★
Current: 1-3
Speciality: A coral garden like no other

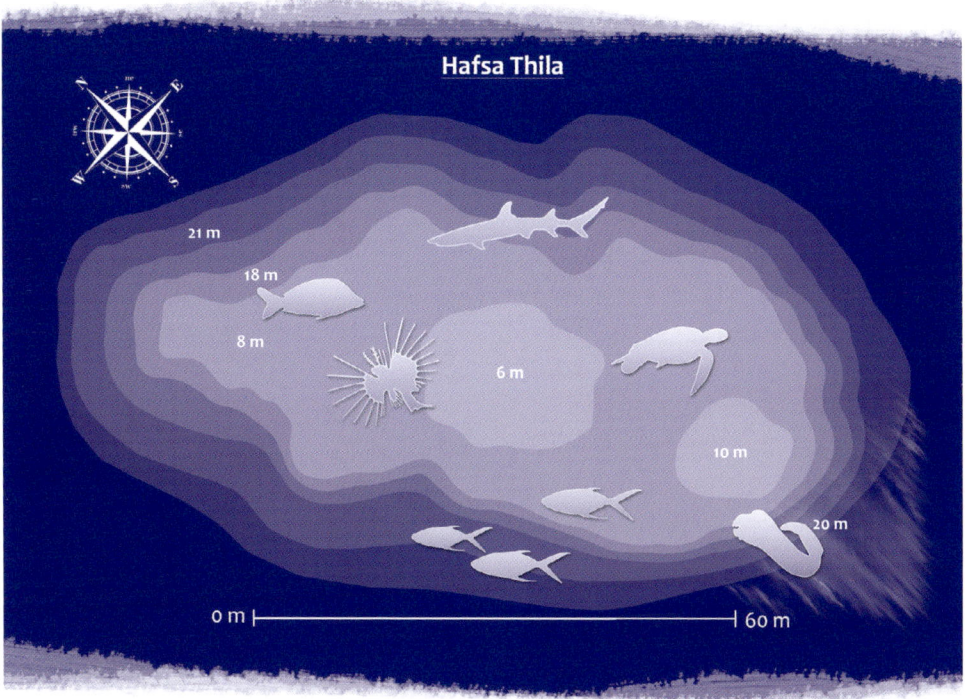

7 – Hafsa Thila

This tiny thila is the treasure of the western Huvadhoo atoll. It measures a mere 70m in diameter and is located very close to the outer atoll ring. Furthermore it is the only elevation of the sea bottom. Fish are normally circling the thila in their thousands, while hundreds are hiding between the few and mostly dead coral blocks. This is because the local fishermen regularly hunt here for their bait fish. They deploy ground nets that destroy fragile corals but make place for faster growing algae. The result is a completely different type of reef in comparison with the other reefs described in this book. At Hafsa Thila it is a must to dig your nose into every little crack of the reef. The attentive eye will spot such rare sights as the extremely well camouflaged scorpion and leaf fish. Just be a little bit careful with the common Bearded Moray at this dive site. The species is far more aggressive than its larger relatives. Also sharks are not as rare as at Hafsa Thila. They often swim between the blocks, which gives you the opportunity to see them more often. Anyway, due to its size you will get round the thila more than once during a dive and so there is more than ample of time to fully investigate the top at around 10m. The current is normally rather mild, but can also be a bit stronger at times. This site is the author's favourite.

N 00.36.500, E 073.08.950
Depth: 10-25m
Fish: ★★★★☆
Corals: ★☆☆☆☆
Current: 1-3
Speciality: Tuna, morays and fish swarms

8 – Meradhoo Kandu

Meradhoo Kandu is something special. During the south-west monsoon it is possible to observe the extremely rare Silver-tip Reef-sharks. Yet another very rare feature of this channel is its coral growth, which reaches all the way down to the bottom at 30m and is entirely covered by corals. If you love corals and always wished to be surrounded by them, then this is the place to dive!

As with any channel, Meradhoo Kandu is best dived during the incoming tide. The dive starts on the south side of the outer reef and leads around the fish-packed corner into the channel.

N 00.36.000, E 073.04.250
Depth: 5-30m
Fish: ★ ★ ★ ★ ★
Corals: ★ ★ ★ ★ ★
Current: 2-4
Speciality: Silver-tip Reef-sharks during south-west monsoon

9 – Meradhoo Thila

This dive site is not one single thila but rather a number of smaller pillars. The location close to Meradhoo Kandu provides fresh oceanic water for pelagic fish like fusiliers. In contrast to its bigger brother, the channel of Meradhoo, the current here is normally weak because of its somewhat set-back position. This makes it the perfect thila for beginners and people who don't like strong currents but always wished to see this kind of reef.

N 00.35.450, E 073.06.650
Depth: 5-30m
Fish: ★ ★ ★ ★ ★
Corals: ★ ★ ★ ★ ★
Current: 1-2
Speciality: Beginner thila with lots of fusiliers

A turtle in space, or dives with Chris

Obviously you dive and see a lot when you work as a marine biologist in the Maldives. However, some dives manage to stick in your memory more than others. In my case, I especially remember those dives that somehow involved personal contact with marine life. In one of the first dives of this kind, my dive buddy Chris met a very curious turtle. The dive itself was nothing too special, up to the point that I turned around to look for Chris who fell a little behind.

What I saw was an image taken straight out of a science fiction film. Chris was vertically hovering motionless in midwater when a small, flat 'starfighter' with huge floppy front wings tried to dock with him, and was slowly drawing nearer. Chris's hand extended towards the turtle in slow-motion. The situation was frozen in time, all movement had ceased.

During this second, I wanted to circle the still couple like the camera in Matrix. It somehow bore an odd resemblance to Michelangelo's fresco in the Sistine Chapel: turtle reaching its beak out to the helpless diver. I don't know what would have happened if they would have touched each other, but I know that it sticks just as much to Chris's memory as in mine.

10 – Cabbage Thila

This thila is located very close to the outer reef and is best dived as if it were a channel during the incoming tide. The dive starts off flat and quickly continues down to a 20m deep plateau. You can follow it for some time until a depth of around 30m, where the plateau drops off to about 40m and stretches into a nearby channel. During the first part especially you should meet many fusiliers, tuna and possibly sea turtles. The fish diversity reduces towards the deeper parts, where you can see sporadic eagle rays. It is replaced by splendid stony coral gardens.

Because of its proximity to the channel the current might turn out much stronger than anticipated. It is therefore at the discretion of the dive guide whether diving is possible on any particular day or not.

N 00.34.350, E 073.05.300
Depth: 5-30m
Fish: ★★★★★
Corals: ★★★★★
Current: 1-3 (4)
Speciality: Coral growth

11 – Haodi Galaa Giri

Haodi Galaa Giri is not too big, maybe 90m in diameter, so it is rather easy to circle the site on a single dive. This offers the possibility of investigating every nook and cranny of the reef and ensures you don't miss any of the big jacks and countless fusiliers that closely circle the reef in huge swarms during a strong current. And because the giri is only 15 minutes by boat away from the atoll ring, the location generates a good water exchange that in turn leads to loads of fish. Also White-tip Reef-sharks, sea turtles and the (elsewhere) rare bannerfish are regularly seen here. Despite the relatively exposed location, the current is comparatively mild, which allows even drift beginners to dive at this spot.

N 00.31.675, E 073.03.450
Depth: 5-30m
Fish: ★★★★★
Corals: ★★★★★
Current: 1-3
Speciality: Huge jack swarms

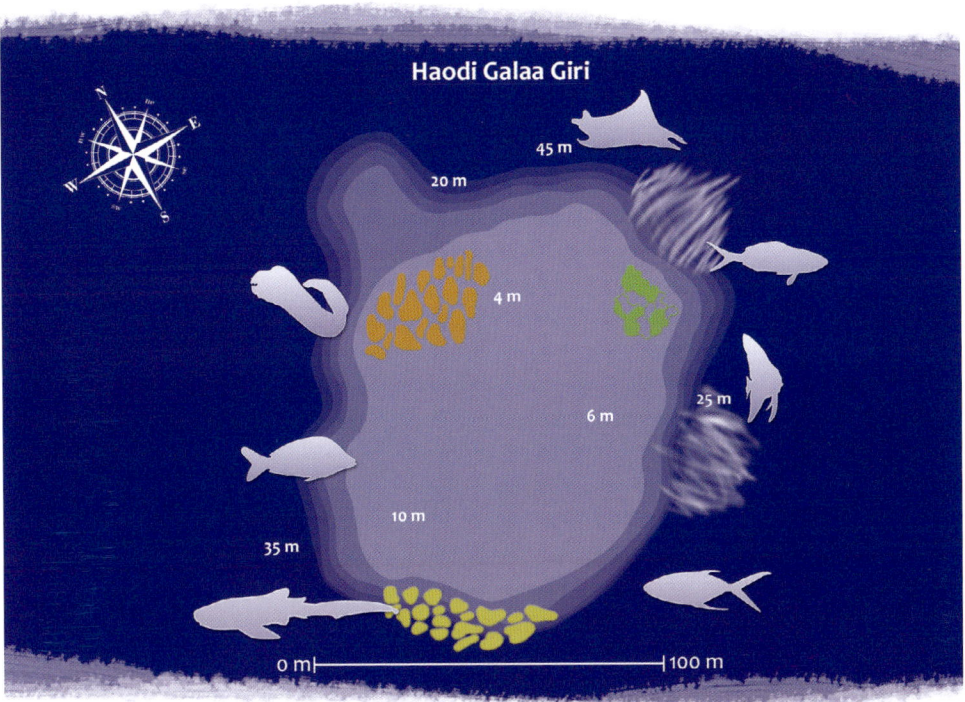

12 – Kafena Kandu

The channel of Kafena is very small but pretty. During the incoming tide it is packed with fish, especially swarming fusiliers, but also snappers, barracudas, porcupinefish and Napoleons. Also sharks are often spotted here, including Grey Reef-sharks and White-tips.

The dive usually starts on the outside reef in the north then leads around the corner and into the narrow channel. Keep your eyes open while diving around the corner, as there are lots of fish to see.

N 00.31.450, E 73.00.000
Depth: 7-30m
Fish: ★★★★★
Corals: ★★★★★
Current: 3-5
Speciality: Great and schooling barracudas and Grey Reef-sharks

13 – Rahadhoo Kandu

Rahadhoo channel is found on the west side of the atoll, south of the main island Thinadhoo. The channel's reef tops at 14m on the outside and becomes shallower when you get into the channel. Fish abundance is very high during incoming tides and attracts schools of barracudas to the seaward opening.
    Depending on the current, the dive starts on the outside in the north or south of the opening, ensuring that you will always get a chance to glimpse one of the corners. This is where fish activity is usually highest. Besides the barracudas you may also see Eagle Rays and sharks. Divers need to be good with their air consumption as it takes about 75 minutes to visit the entire dive site.

N 00.30.750, E 073.00.000
Depth: 14-30m
Fish: ★ ★ ★ ★ ☆
Corals: ★ ★ ☆ ☆ ☆
Current: 2-5
Speciality: Schools of barracudas

14 – Kaadedhdhoo Kandu

This channel features an atypically gently sloping reef structure. Probably as a result of its vicinity to more densely populated islands, the coral abundance and their growth is comparatively low. Fish, however, are more abundant, especially during strong incoming tides. Mantas are seldom seen and usually only during the rainy season. Nevertheless, at this time, it is the only known spot in west Huvadhoo where these elegant giants may be observed.

N 00.28.500, E 073.00.000
Depth: 15-30m
Fish: ★ ★ ★ ☆ ☆
Corals: ★ ☆ ☆ ☆ ☆
Current: 3-5
Speciality: Occasional manta sightings during rainy season (May-September)

Sea dogs, or dives with Michael

Dives with Michael always meant one never dived alone. Not that he had a split personality or anything, no nothing like that. Rather, he had the gift of attracting marine life.

Michael was an ambitious and skilled diver who wanted to circum-dive the entire island before the end of his 10-day stay. Now islands in the Maldives are not exactly famous for their vast size. The island of Funamaudoo is no exception and thus it was a fairly reasonable plan. Usually, he stood on the sill of our dive school a moment after we had opened. Because he was such an easy going and undemanding dive guest as well as person, diving with him was always good fun.

To start the morning with a fun dive really made my day. We quickly buckled up and trotted to the point we had exited the water the day before, clipped on our fins, spat in our masks and lost ourselves in the silence of the sea. We always chose a very comfortable pace and a moderate depth in order to enjoy every second and stretch our time under water. His gift usually started working immediately after we had entered the water. We had not even reached a depth of 5m before his best friends approached, happily waving their tails at him, remoras.

I saw many other divers that reacted in panic, kicking themselves all the way up to the surface while trying to hit the fish with their fins, until they shot out of the water like Flipper. Not so Michael. Instead he started playing with them and only after the dive complained a little that 'Killer' had bitten him again today. The remoras often followed him all the way to the beach into ankle deep water. They just loved him (You can see a remora attached to Michael's nitrox tank on page 141).

15 – Dhevva Thila

This thila is located directly next to Dhevva Giri and lifts its top up to just 18m below the surface. Hence, it is a rather deep dive site, which makes Nitrox your first choice. Once you get down though there are many fish to see, especially the (elsewhere) rarely seen batfish, which occur here even in schools. Giant groupers are found hiding under coral blocks together with myriads of glass fish, whilst elegant Rainbow Runners swim in large swarms through the open water. Mobulas also fly by regularly.

    This very small thila measures only 40m in diameter, allowing divers to comfortably circle the site more than once during a single dive and spiralling their way upwards. The current usually stays within moderate limits and only the depth restricts this site for really advanced divers.

N 00.35.350, E 73.15.650
Depth: 18-30m
Fish: ★★ ★ ★ ★
Corals: ★★★ ★ ★
Current: 2-3
Speciality: Batfish in schools

Dhevva

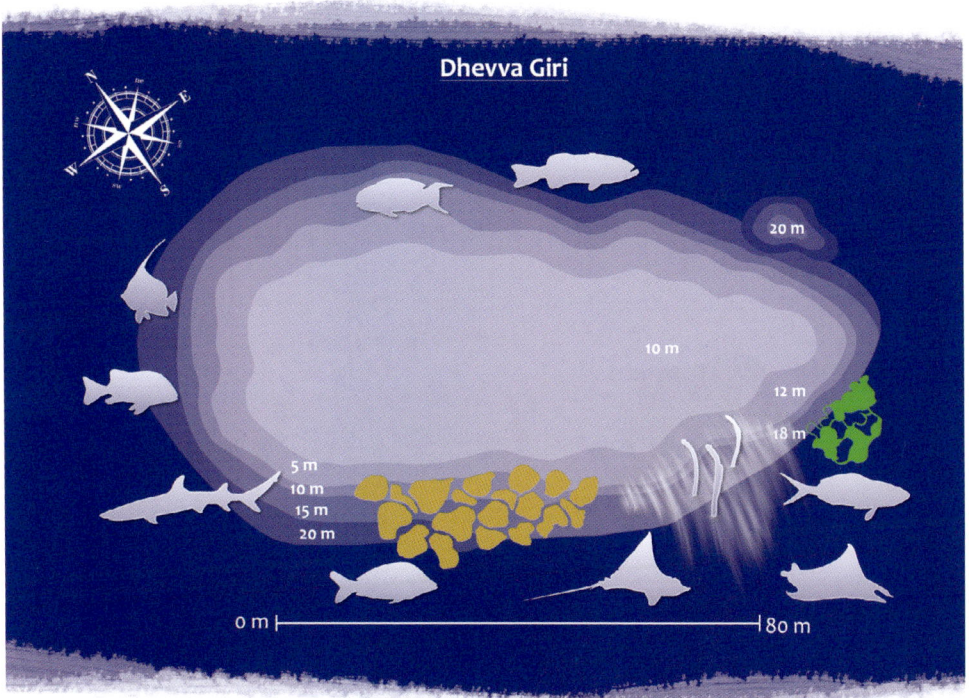

16 – Dhevva Giri

Dhevva Giri is the classical giri of the area with beautiful coral that can be almost circled in a single dive. It sets the benchmark for all other giris. The current can become a little stronger from time to time but usually remains within the scope of advanced dive beginners. It is therefore a very good dive site for an introduction to drift diving in the Maldives. Huge swarms of fusiliers are regularly present and circle divers. Big coral blocks stand in the gently sloping reef and are often entirely filled up with glass fish. If you look inside the small caves you can sometimes startle big groupers and Sabre Squirrelfish. Along the western edge below 20m, the reef suddenly drops down to 30m. The resulting wall offers a grand stage for sea fans and whips, and sharks are often seen at this corner. During the late north-east monsoon (March/April), Dhevva Giri offers another attraction: above the southern sand flats you can see mobulas in groups of around a dozen or so animals.

N 00.35.350, E 73.15.650
Depth: 5-30m
Fish: ★★★☆☆
Corals: ★★☆☆☆
Current: 1-3
Speciality: Regular sightings of White-tip Reef-sharks and eagle rays

17 – Dhevvamaagalaa Faru

Dhevvamaagalaa has never disappointed a diver. There is always something memorable about every single dive here. The reef offers White-tip Reef-sharks, sea turtles, lionfish, fusiliers and jacks. Often you will see a great many interesting species during a single dive. The less common species like Giant Moray, pufferfish and stingrays make it worth visiting this place again. Which side of the island you dive on depends solely on the prevailing current. It can already be a bit stronger because of the island's relatively close location to the atoll ring. On the other hand, this is good place to practice for later drift dives in the extreme currents of channels.

N 00.34.450, E 073.11.475
Depth: 5-30m
Fish: ★★★☆☆
Corals: ★★★☆☆
Current: 1-3
Speciality: Very balanced dive, never disappointing

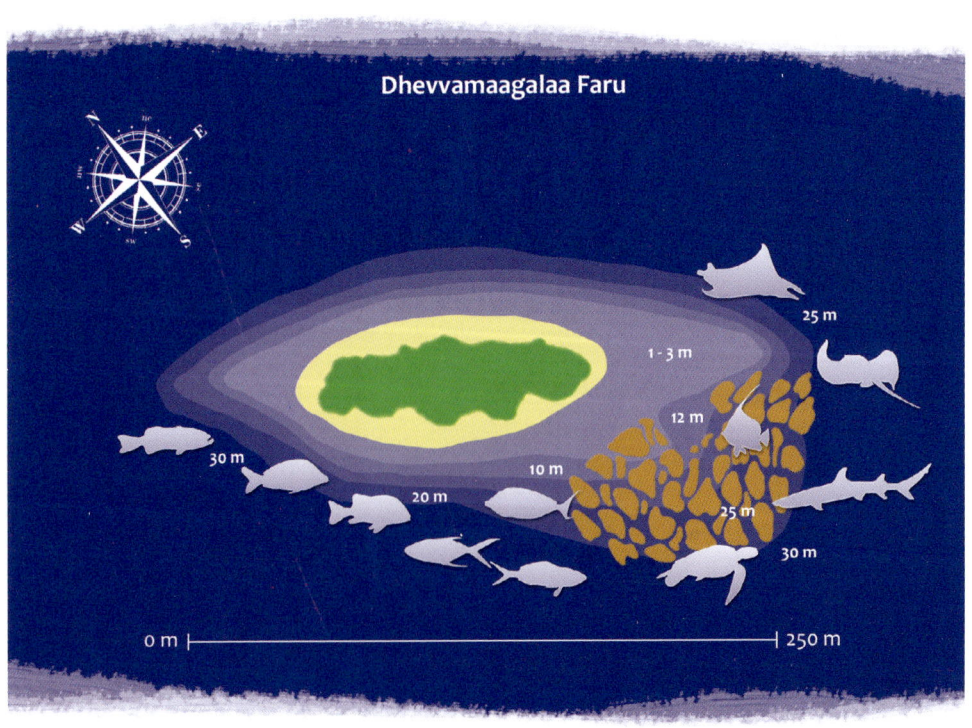

Dhevvamaagalaa

18 – Funamaudoo – Club Robinson Maldives
House Reef

The island of Funamaudoo is around 650m in length and thus comparatively long. Accordingly, this large house reef hosts a vast array of different coral reef habitats. The long north-east side is most exposed to the weather, which is clearly visible from its narrow lagoon (the water between beach and reef). During days with strong current you can find thousands of fusiliers hunting for plankton, also sea turtles, snappers, batfish and even mobulas are abundant during such conditions.

Further towards the north-west tip of the island, the reef top and lagoon stretch to their widest extent. Around the tip is the best point to spot the two (at the time of writing) large residential Napoleons of the resort. There are also reports of Leopard, Nurse and Grey Reef-sharks from early morning (sunrise!!!) dives and snorkelling tours, the time when these large predators retreat from hunting. The north-western tip of the reef is especially pleasant if the current is directly hitting against it. You can almost be sure to see sharks.

Further around, along the south-western coast, the reef becomes somewhat less exciting but sometimes offers extremely rare sights of Flying Gurnards and Ghost Pipefish. The local dive school can be found on this side of the island, which is why the obligatory check dives are done here. It is also on this side where two Giant Leaf Fish hide in their cave and can be readily visited during the first dive. Lastly, at the south-eastern tip of the island you will enter the realm of the Red Basses. These large snappers are always seen around this end of the island. A special treat are the local remoras that will immediately try to attach themselves to you, assuming you to be a Whale Shark! If they become too pesky, try to punch them with your hand at close range. Their reflexes are limited.

The current around Funamaudoo can vary from mild to strong. Strength and direction change with season.

N 00.31.939, E 073.11.428
Depth: 5-30m
Fish: ★★★☆☆
Corals: ★★★☆☆
Current: 1-3
Speciality: High diversity and sticky remoras

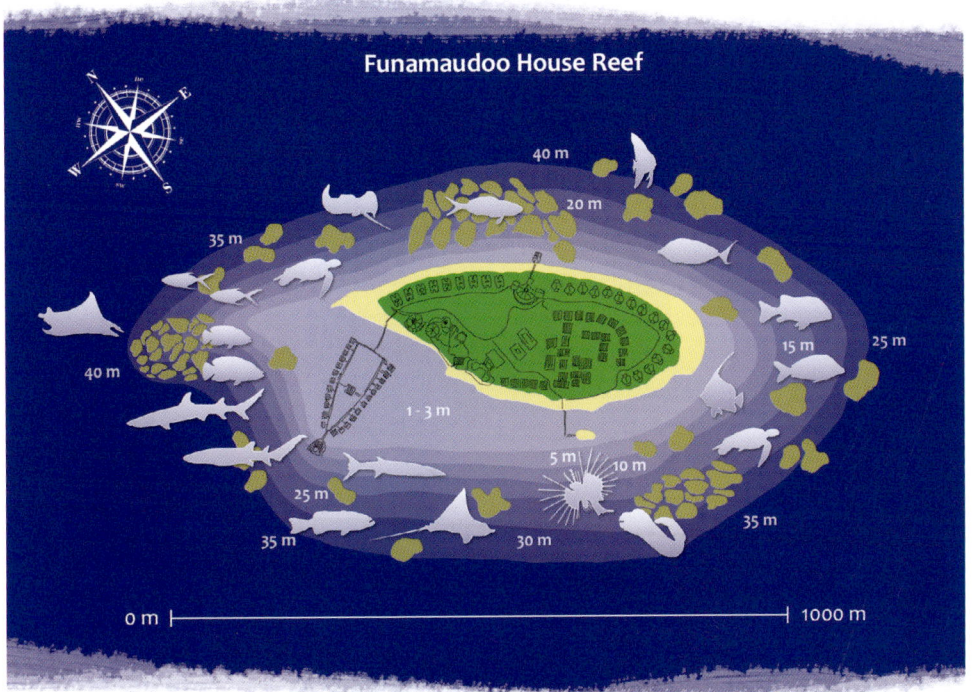

19 – Hagedhoo Faru

The reef around the island of Hagedhoo is a true paradise for snorkellers and is a really good dive site. There are many large corals that lift their dead heads above the surface and can thus be investigated by snorkellers to the fullest. Besides hermit crabs, you will find many different sea urchins and sea cucumbers, whilst brightly coloured nudibranches are common. The impressive Slate-pencil Sea Urchins seem to be especially fond of this reef. It is the author's favourite snorkelling spot.

    Depending on the regularly light current, divers start from the northeast corner and drift in a westerly direction. At depths below 15m, dense swarms of Blue-striped Snappers, tunas, Spotted Unicornfish and fusiliers can be found. Even mobulas, the small brothers of the manta, have been observed here.

N 00.01.219, E 073.12.810
Depth: 5-30m
Fish: ★★☆☆☆
Corals: ★★★☆☆
Current: 1-2
Speciality: Blue-striped Snapper and Slate-pencil Sea Urchins

20 – Hirifushi Faru

Hirifushi is an unusual reef. The wide sand flats between free-standing coral blocks leave room for flounders, Garden Eels and bivalves, thereby creating a nutrition base completely different from that usually found in Huvadhoo. Stingrays are expected and are a common sight once this reef is investigated a little further. But besides these the free-standing coral heads make it a worthwhile dive. Due to their location in the sand (see picture of *Porites lobata* on page 79) even divers with a less than perfect buoyancy can leave their legs on the ground and investigate the blocks at very close range.

N 00.31.485, E 73.24.390
Depth: 5-25m
Fish: ★ ☆ ☆ ☆ ☆
Corals: ★ ★ ★ ☆ ☆
Current: 1-2
Speciality: Wide sand flats with free-standing coral blocks

21 – Gosi Faru

The reef around the island of Gosi seems to attract White-tip Reef-sharks. Even snorkellers regularly spot this species. Also small groups of young Grey Reef-sharks have been seen here, whilst sea turtles can often also be observed paddling through the gentle to moderate current. The corals of this site are somewhat limited to the upper 10m, which makes this site a perfect snorkelling spot.

N 00.30.457, E 073.08.831
Depth: 5-30m
Fish: ★ ★ ★ ★ ☆
Corals: ★ ★ ☆ ☆ ☆
Current: 1-2
Speciality: White-tip Reef-sharks and sea turtles

22 – Leon's Giri

Leon Giri is slightly smaller than Dhevva Giri and not as deep, as the position of coral is concentrated to the upper areas. Here you will often find big spiny lobsters under the coral heads. Normally you can circle the spot in a single dive. At the lower ends of the slope are wide sandy areas where Garden Eels are seen holding their heads into the current. The current is a lot weaker than at Dhevva Giri, due to its position further inside of the atoll. This is why the dive site is especially suitable for younger and less experienced divers who want to see a giri. The name of the giri derives from a bright and keen 11-year-old diver from Germany, Leon.

N 00.28.600, E 073.11.750
Depth: 5-20m
Fish: ★★★ ★ ★
Corals: ★★ ★ ★ ★
Current: 1-2
Speciality: Rock lobsters and garden eels

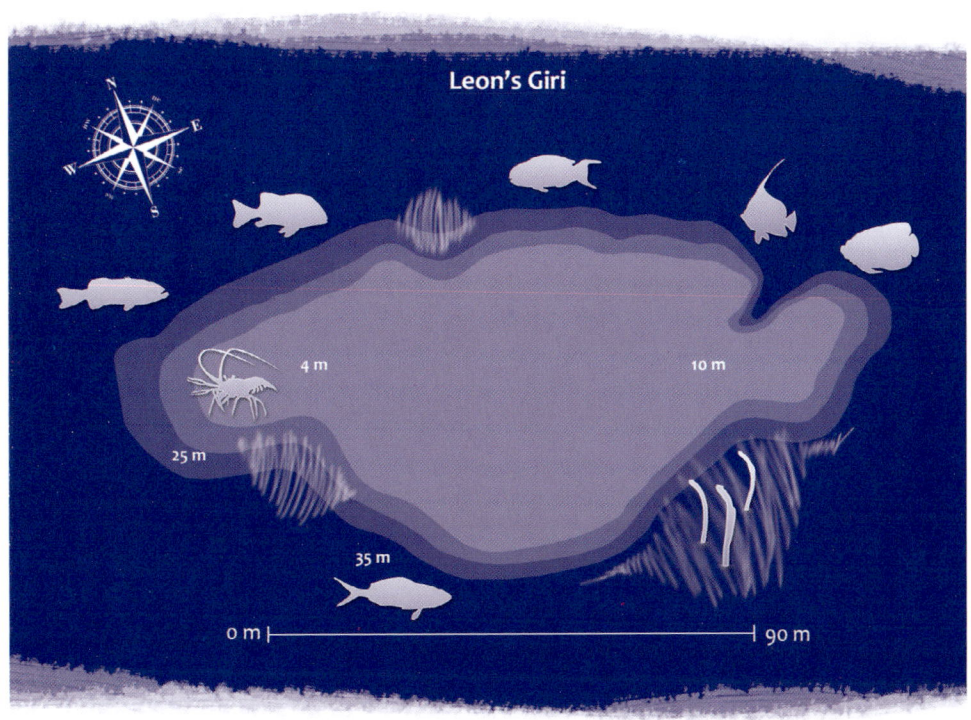

23 – Baulhageella Faru

Baulhageella will charm every diver with its exquisite stone corals. Immense table corals stand right next to massive *Porites* species. Glass fish scrimmage in their little caves. The current is rather mild around the island and makes it the perfect training ground for dive beginners. Just make sure to take a look under the larger coral blocks. You will very often find lionfish hiding here. Snorkellers especially will spend many memorable hours at this location.

N 00.29.359, E 073.10.385
Depth: 5-30m
Fish: ★★☆☆☆
Corals: ★★★★☆
Current: 1-2
Speciality: Corals in perfect condition

24 – Kuda Giri

Kuda Giri is especially suitable for dive students. The current is weak, but the dive site already gives the feeling of diving on a really wild reef in the forgotten seas of Huvadhoo. Bodu Giri and Leon's Giri are just around the corner. Together they make for a great day diving for beginners. The divemaster or instructor will most likely include at least one of the corners of the Giri, as most of the fish can be found there. This usually means that divers have to swim against the mild current at the beginning of the dive before finding themselves gently floating along behind the corner.

N 00.28.700, E 073.11.650
Depth: 5-25m
Fish: ★★☆☆☆
Corals: ★★★☆☆
Current: 1-3
Speciality: Easy diving, perfect for students

25 – Bodu Giri

Bodu Giri is located south-west of Leon's Giri and is slightly larger. The current is mostly rather strong, but still moderate enough to allow less experienced divers to have an enjoyable time. Most dives at this site start against the current, allowing you to dive entirely around one of the two corners. The coral growth there is particularly beautiful. Also there are usually lots of fish drifting with the current whilst feeding on plankton. Sharks are regularly sighted and also eagle rays seem to like this spot as they are often seen there.

N 00.27.325, E 073.14.090
Depth: 5-25m
Fish: ★★ ★ ★ ★
Corals: ★★★ ★ ★
Current: 1-3
Speciality: Eagle Rays and huge Red Bass

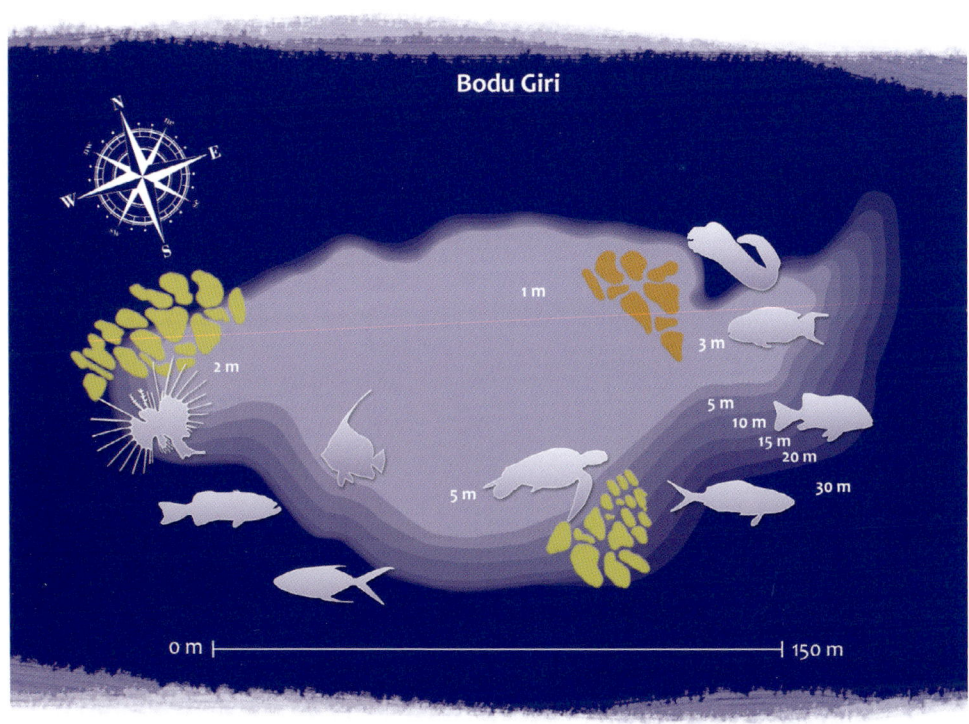

26 – Beyru Ha Thila

This thila may be very small but it provides a stunning diversity for its size. Big coral blocks are spread all over the site at different depths, which offer different species their preferred habitats. The thila also attracts sharks, even Grey Reef-sharks, which is a rather rare sight inside the atoll. Diving Beyru Ha usually means having to circle the small thila at least once before you gradually swim towards the reef top. On the way up, divers are well advised to stop at a large coral block about 14m to the west. This block is home to beautiful pink anemones and their clownfish sidekicks.

N 00.25.800, E 073.11.750
Depth: 8-30m
Fish: ★★★★☆
Corals: ★★★☆☆
Current: 2-4
Speciality: Hunting jacks and pink anemones

29 – Nilandhoo Thila

If you love corals this is one of the places you absolutely have to dive on in Huvadhoo. The entire thila feels like a maze made up of corals through which you have to find your way. The weak current plays along and makes for a very relaxing dive. The abundance of fish is rather low; however, just take a look under some of the beautiful coral heads – you never know what you may find. It is also a very good dive site for a second dive during a safari to the eastern atoll ring.

N 00.36.700, E 073.26.450
Depth: 5-30m
Fish: ★☆☆☆☆
Corals: ★★★★★
Current: 1-2
Speciality: Stunning coral maze

27 – Villingili Kandu

The near-by tuna factory guarantees a high abundance of fish, especially barracudas, which seem to be very fond of this site. They regularly occur here in large swarms that circle in the classical cylinder formation below the surface. A truly majestic sight. Also the above average appearance of large turtles characterises this dive site. Naturally, sharks are also attracted by the fish residues from the factory. As it is usual for channels and depending on the tide, the current can be very strong. For this reason, this site is recommended for experienced divers only.

N 00.44.850, E 073.26.250
Depth: 15-30m
Fish: ★★★★☆
Corals: ★★☆☆☆
Current: 2-5
Speciality: Many sea turtles and barracudas

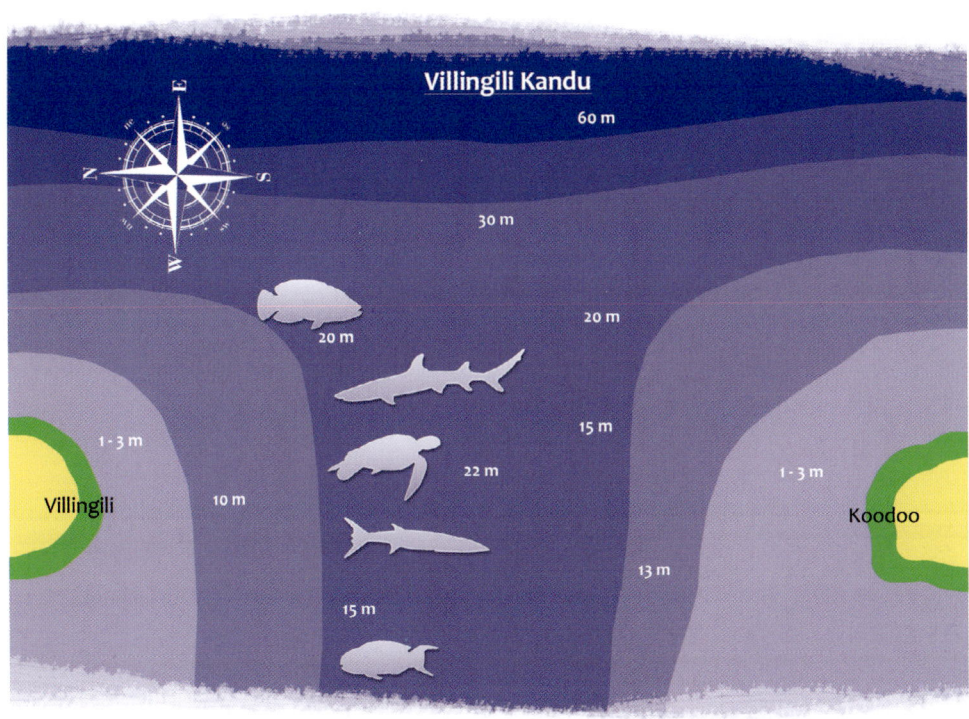

28 – Nilandhoo Kandu

The channel at Nilandhoo is a true paradise for divers who have come to Huvadhoo first and foremost to see sharks. The dive begins at the north side of the outer reef. During the usually very strong current, a rapid descent is mandatory. Sometimes even negative descents (descents right after jumping into the water) are recommended in order not to miss the nice spots. Once in the water, you descend to 20m following the current towards the corner, while slowly descending further to 30m. Somewhat before the corner is already a good place to see some sharks. Directly at the corner you will see the sharks holding station effortlessly in the current, waiting for prey. The mostly crystal clear water allows you to watch from as far as 40m and there is no other place like this to watch them.

After 10 to 15 minutes of this shark-watching let the incoming current take over which allows you to drift into the channel. During the drift it is advisable to work your way north-west slightly across the current in order to take a glimpse at the beautiful corals on the inside of the channel.

The current is almost always really strong at Nilandhoo and will challenge even the most experienced diver. Furthermore, because of the long times spent at the bottom for the shark observation and often following dives, Nitrox is highly recommended. This is no place for beginners, but certainly a favourite channel of the author.

N 00.38.100, E 073.27.300
Depth: 20-30m
Fish: ★★★★☆
Corals: ★★☆☆☆
Current: 2-5
Speciality: White-tip and Grey Reef-sharks

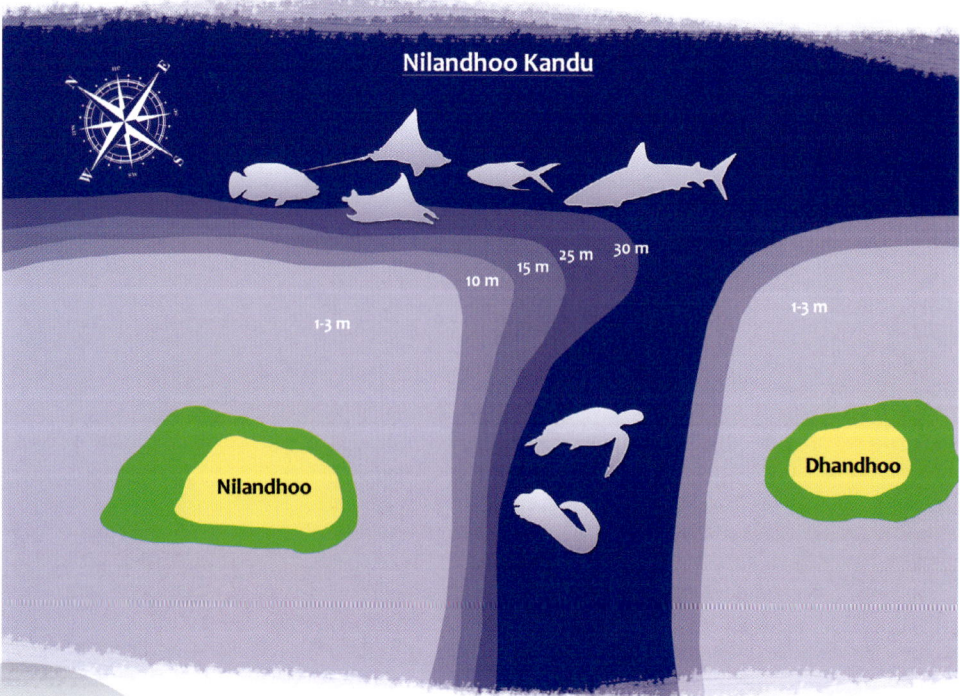

30 – Vodamulaa Kandu

You will almost certainly have met sharks already at 25m, so Vodamulaa Kandu is the perfect site for a second channel dive. The elegant predators are hunting at the corner of the channel for smaller fish. Somewhat before the corner, the reef features a huge cavern-like structure at around 25m, Vodamulaa Cave. On a dive coming from the northern outer reef, you can rest here for a while to observe sharks before advancing to the corner and into the channel. Close to the bottom and across the current you approach the northern reef. Often full-grown Green Turtles can be seen here swimming in the current, whilst huge groupers are hiding between the corals. There are also many species of fish that cannot be seen inside of the atoll. Good examples are the Threespot and Yellowface Angelfish and otherwise seldom seen soft corals are a common sight.

Strong currents also restrict this channel to experienced divers and make Nitrox a sensible choice, especially during a second dive.

N 00.35.800, E 073.29.800
Depth: 15-25 (30) m
Fish: ★★★★☆
Corals: ★★☆☆☆
Current: 2-5
Speciality: White-tip and Grey Reef-sharks

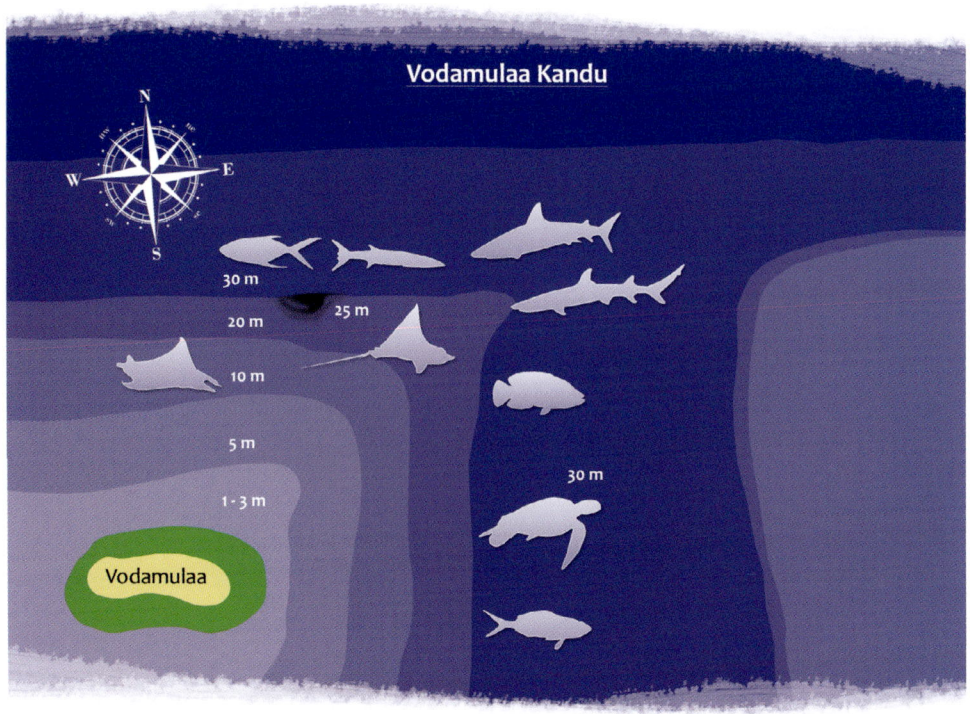

A director down under, or dives with JP

JP was the director of the resort and a divemaster at the same time. I had the chance to dive with him on various occasions but one dive stands out. It was the first night dive we had organised for our guests, but it was also the first Maldivian night dive arranged for us personally. It was to become an unforgettable experience.

We started the dive from the quay of the resort. Already gearing up and listening to the briefing by Julia, the instructor, was good fun, and the fish in the water looked very promising. We all jumped straight from the quay. JP was the first and immediately spotted the first shark. It didn't take long until the rest of the group joined him. JP and I were a buddy team and as experienced divers we took the rear of the group. As we descended we saw the first shark, the second for JP, by the fading light of the moon.

We had agreed to a depth of no more than 15m and enjoyed our dive between sleeping fish that we could approach at very close range. In contrast to the sleeping fish, the plankton came alive and started blinking when we agitated the water. When I was just swirling the water again to provoke a display of bioluminescent fireworks, a shadow passed the edge of my field of vision. I whirled around and saw a shark only 3m away, gently gliding through coral heads. When it was about 7m behind the group, it turned around and swam in a descending line directly towards me. It was a small White-tip Reef-shark, but my heart made a little jump anyway. It passed right below my angled legs and lifted fins. JP was directly behind me but about 2m deeper and so the shark passed by him right in front of his chest. The next seconds elapsed in slow-motion. The shark described a soft half circle with its gently waving tail fin, whereupon JP careful reached out his hand and finally touched it. The shark disappeared in the dark and left me completely baffled. Looking at JP, I could see the big grin behind his mouthpiece. The jealous marine biologist in me was raving.

It only took him another five minutes until he found for himself the next marine friends, two squid. I don't know why these usually very shy creatures didn't fly past him but they didn't. I witnessed a mutual play of utmost curiosity, on one side a resort director, behaving like an absent-minded five-year old, acting like a squid with his fingers in front of his mouth, and on the other hand a real squid seemingly trying to communicate with softly swaying tentacles. It was both hilarious and magical at the same time: the floating, colour changing squid in the midst of darkness only partially illuminated and this clumsy bubbling human.

JP was still smiling from one ear to the other when we left the water.

31 – Mareeha Kandu

If you want to see an armada of Grey Reef-sharks, you need to dive at Mareeha Kandu. And if the weather and tide conditions permit, you might find yourself crossing the channel, facing up to 100 sharks. Breathtaking. But even during less fortunate days you will easily observe 30 to 50 sharks at one time. Also large squadrons of Eagle Rays are commonly seen here. Reliable dive guides of the area report pods of 40 animals gently flying above their heads. Next to large groups of stunning marine life, the dive spot also features the usual suspects of channels: Large White-tip Reef-sharks, fast swimming tunas and jacks, as well as large groupers and turtles. In short: this place is a must-see!

    As usual, the dive starts from either the north or south entrance of the channel from the outside of the reef. The difference of Mareeha to other channels is the possibility of crossing the channel if the tide permits. In this case, you follow the reef's drop off over to the other side instead of the reef's bending profile towards the inside of the channel. Either dive will be unforgettable.

N 00.33.180, E 073.31.840
Depth: 15-30m
Fish: ★★★★★
Corals: ★★☆☆☆
Current: 3-5
Speciality: Many Grey Reef-sharks (30-100!) in the same field of vision

32 – Kondey Kandu

The channel of Kondey is at the far east of the atoll and features a sloping reef with a sharp drop-off at 30m down to about 60m. Ridges like these are perfect spots to observe sharks that hunt in the up-welling waters during incoming tides. The only thing divers have to do is hold onto some dead piece of coral and let the current be the director of this submarine odyssey. On the other hand, a diver might find their vision hampered by immensely large and dense schools of fusiliers that commonly occur in Kondey. Another very rare speciality here is the coral garden at the bottom of the channel, a truly remarkable sight and extremely uncommon for other channels of the area.

    The dive in Kondey Kandu can be started from the north or the south side. The decision of the divemaster is usually based on experience about the local conditions and the tidal situation. Both sides feature a similar rich underwater world.

N 00.29.350, E 073.33.500
Depth: 10-30m
Fish: ★★★★☆
Corals: ★★★★☆
Current: 3-5
Speciality: Gigantic, dense clouds of fusiliers and a channel bottom entirely filled by corals

33 – Mafzoo Giri

Mafzoo Giri might be quite a small place but offers a lot for its size. Right at the start of a dive, you should descend on the south side into a jungle of large gorgonians that spread their maze-structured fans into the current. Because the giri is so small, you won't have any difficulties swimming around it during your dive. This is very good as the next attraction is waiting for you on the north side. Here you will find a large coral block at around 15m that hosts no less then six residing leaf fishes behind a dizzying wall of glass fish. A very nice dive spot.

N 00.20.150, E 073.26.850
Depth: 5-30m
Fish: ★ ★ ★ ★ ★
Corals: ★ ★ ★ ☆ ☆
Current: 2-4
Speciality: Gorgonians and leaf fish

34 – Vadhoo Thila

Vadhoo Thila is a long reef that bustles with fish of all kinds. It is very likely that you will see everything from large fusilier swarms, Napoleons, turtles, tunas, White-tip Reef-sharks and Eagle Rays on a single dive. Even Grey Reef-sharks have occasionally been seen here. Another nice aspect is the possibility of ending it on top of the thila itself, hovering above a garden of table corals. Because of all these riches, even safari boats often bring their guests to this dive site.

N 00.14.400, E 073.16.590
Depth: 5-30m
Fish: ★ ★ ★ ★ ☆
Corals: ★ ★ ★ ☆ ☆
Current: 2-4
Speciality: Numerous fish of many kinds

Chapter 3

Identification guide

Groups index

68	Algae
70	Siliceous sponges
72	Stingers
73	Soft coral
75	Hexacorallia
77	Hard coral
84	Softies – Molluscs
85	Bivalves
87	Univalves
89	Octopuses
90	Crustaceans
92	Spiny fellows – Echinoderms
93	Sea lilies or feather stars
95	Sea stars
99	Sea urchins
101	Sea cucumbers
103	Chordates
104	Sea squirts

Cartilaginous fish

110	Nurse sharks
111	Zebra sharks
112	Whale sharks
113	Requiem sharks
115	Stingrays
117	Eagle rays

Boney fish

120	Moray eels
122	Garden eels
123	Lizardfish
124	Needlefish
125	Soldier- and squirrelfish
126	Pipefish
127	Trumpetfish
128	Cornetfish
129	Lion- and scorpionfish
130	Sea bass
130	Soapfish
131	Basslets
132	Groupers
135	Bigeyes
136	Cardinalfish
139	Jacks and travellies
141	Remoras
142	Snappers
144	Fusiliers
146	Pursemouths
147	Sweetlips
148	Threadfin bream
149	Emperors
150	Goatfish
152	Rudderfish
153	Butterflyfish
159	Angelfish
160	Hawkfish
162	Damselfish
167	Wrasses
171	Parrotfish
173	Sandperch
174	Blennies
176	Triplefins
177	Gobies
180	Batfish
181	Rabbitfish
182	Moorish idols
183	Surgeonfish
186	Barracudas
187	Mackerels and tuna
188	Lefteye flounder
189	Boxfish
190	Triggerfish
192	Filefish
193	Pufferfish
194	Porcupinefish
195	Sea turtles
197	Dolphins

Reef symbioses

Some of the most peculiar and interesting things to observe in tropical reefs are the various relationships, i.e. symbioses, between different animals and plants. The quality of these partnerships range from one-sided disadvantageous parasitism, to mutual two-sided advantageous, true symbiosis.

The list presented here is by no means complete; it merely attempts to demonstrate some of the more common partnerships that can be observed. The most important symbiosis in tropical reefs is the one between corals and their incorporated single-celled algae, i.e. endosymbiotic zooxanthellae. This particular true symbiosis is not included in this list as it is fully covered in the chapter on stony corals.

Mutualism – symbiosis in its best sense

Gobies and burrowing shrimps

Gobies are bottom dwellers and many species build their own caves in the sand. However, some apparently more lazy species have outsourced this job to shrimps, while specialising themselves in the job of being watchdog.
    The character of this rather odd couple is of truly mutual benefit. While the shrimp constructs its common safe harbour, the goby sits at the entrance and warns the shrimp of danger by flipping its tail whenever it comes out to deposit some building rubble. The advantage for the shrimp is the protection of the much keener-eyed goby, compared to its own poor vision. The goby gets a safe home and place to breed its offspring.
    Divers can find such happy couples in sandy areas between coral heads at depths between 5-15m.

Cleaner shrimps, wrasses and fish

Cleaning reef species, such as cleaner shrimps and cleaner wrasses, fulfil an enormously important function within the reef ecosystem. As their name suggests, they clean cohabitants of their parasites and dead skin fragments. For this reason they are also often referred to as the hygienic police of the reef. The mutual benefits are rather obvious: while the cleaning species feed on the parasites, the recipients enjoy the grooming and reduced threat of infections. To the system they offer a buffer to the spread of diseases.

Divers, as well as snorkellers, can find them at any depth down to about 30m. To find cleaner shrimps you have to look under coral heads, into little holes and caves.

Clownfish and anemones

People may argue that this is not a true mutual relationship, as the clownfish seems to be the single beneficiary. The protection provided by the anemone's poisonous tentacles is certainly of an immense advantage to the fish and its spawn. However, the fish pays back its host by providing several services. It circulates the water thereby increasing the oxygen supply, cleans the tentacles from uneaten food residues and eats dead tentacles. Obviously this is also to the advantage of the fish as it is thus provided with food in this way. Furthermore, it is believed that the fish attracts unwary prey fish towards the anemone.

In the end, it can be concluded that this relationship is indeed mutual, resulting in a very effective exchange of services that has advantages for both parties. A truly admirable couple.

Commensalism – one-sided advantage

Crown-of-thorns Sea Star and Cardinalfish

The Crown-of-thorns Sea Star is one of the most voracious predators of corals. In large numbers they can transform a flourishing coral reef into a desert within months and hence constitute one of the single greatest threats to reefs in general. Nevertheless, they provide shelter for an inconspicuous Crown-of-thorns Cardinalfish, *Siphamia fuscolineata*. The tiny fish can only be found as a commensal between the spines of the Sea Star and has never been observed in open water. Obviously, the poisonous spines provide perfect protection from being eaten.

This relationship does not represent a true mutual symbiosis, as the Sea Star neither gains an advantage nor a disadvantage from the fish. Therefore, this type of symbiosis is called commensalism.

Groupers and trumpetfish

Another example of a one-sided relationship is the unlikely combination of groupers and trumpetfish, two predators hunting side by side. Whilst the grouper does not seem to have a serious disadvantage from this combination, the trumpetfish makes good use of the larger partner by using it to hide from prey. Divers are well advised to hold still and observe this couple for a while when seen, as it is not the most common sight and quite entertaining. The trumpetfish usually swims above the grouper, suddenly dashing forward to attack its prey. This relationship is not really a true commensalism as the partnership is only temporary when the two fish, by chance, meet each other. Also the trumpet fish does not depend on the grouper for survival or reproduction.

Remoras on large fish... and divers

This relationship is a bit of a special case as remoras can only be considered commensals with some difficulty. Biologists usually sort them into a subcategory of commensalism, called phoresy. This type of symbiosis refers to species that use their hosts exclusively for transportation. In fact, they are hitchhikers. However, the exclusiveness of this definition confronts us with some problems, as remoras do not only hitch a ride.

Remoras also have qualities as mutualists and parasites. They have been observed to feed on their host's faeces as well as enter its gill cavities, supposedly in order to clean them, e.g. on Whale Sharks. This would qualify them as mutualistic. On the other hand, other species do not need them for this service, e.g. mantas, as they regularly visit cleaning stations. For them, remoras are more likely parasites that only increase their drag and hence energy demands. Their sucking plates also likely leave painful marks.

Finally, when remoras meet divers they are quickly regarded as pesky little creatures. The best thing to do is to simply ignore them and, as recommended by Douglas Adams, don't panic! They might upset your nerves but they are certainly not dangerous.

Parasitism – one-sided disadvantage

Fish lice on fish

These parasites can quite often be observed in coral reefs. The easiest way to see them is to watch out for intermediate-sized swarming fish that are locally restricted to larger blocks of coral, such as anthias. The opportunity to see them here is higher. To actually find the lice in the bustle, just look out for awkwardly moving individual fish with dark blotches either behind the head or just in front of the tail fin.

Obviously, this relationship is to the single benefit of the lice and clear disadvantage to the fish. Depending on the exact lice species, they feed on scales, fish mucus, or even directly on the fish's circulatory system.

Algae

Lat: Algae / Deu: Algen

Algae are the plants of the sea. Without them, nothing would work on this planet. It is the phytoplankton that generate up to 80% of the atmosphere's oxygen. This process happens mostly around the poles and only to a moderate extent along the equator. No book about the biology of the sea would be complete without them; however, because phytoplankton are rather difficult to see with a regular diving mask, there are only some larger species shown here. The picture of red algae reveals nicely how gas is produced under water. The other two species are green algae. Pom Pom Algae can be found literally everywhere in the Maldives. The Sailor's Eyeball is rarely seen, at least in the area of Huvadhoo. This species consists of only a single giant cell, which makes it the largest single-celled organism in the world. It is firmly attached to the ground by fine rhizoids and has to be handled delicately when touched, as the carbon-monoxide-filled bubble is rather fragile.

Lat: *Rhodophyta* sp.
Eng: unknown red algae
Deu: unbekannte Rotalge
Size: patchy

Lat: *Tydemania expeditionis*
Eng: Pom Pom Algae
Deu: Flaschenbürstenalge
Size: up to 12cm

Lat: *Valonia ventricosa*
Eng: Sailor's Eyeball Algae
Deu: Meertraube
Size: up to 5cm

Siliceous sponges

Lat: Porifera, Demospongiae / Deu: Hornkieselschwämme

Sponges might look like plants but they are actually animals, the most basic multicellular animal life form on the planet to be exact. They are probably also the oldest, as some fossil records date back as much as 650 million years. Basically, sponges consist of numerous mouths (the pores) that join straight away into the stomach, which forms the channel system that makes up the rest of the body. They feed on whatever drifts through them with the help of collar cells that generate a soft current using their filaments. The very same cells also trap the food items. However, there are other feeding modes. As the name suggests, the Coral-eating Sponge feeds on corals (see picture). It simply wraps them up and starts digesting. All species shown here belong to the family of Demospongiae. This family contains siliceous spicules, small spine-like structures that provide stability, rather than calcareous spicules, which are the characteristic feature of the second family, Calcarea.

Lat: *Paratetilla bacca*
Eng: Berry Sponge
Deu: Beeren-Schwamm
Size: up to 6cm

Porifea Chapter 3 — Identification guide

Lat: *Spheciospongia cf. vagabunda*
Eng: Vagabond Sponge
Deu: Vagabunden Schwamm
Size: depends on host

Lat: *Haliclona nematifera*
Eng: Coral-eating Sponge
Deu: Korallenfressender Schwamm
Size: depends on host

Lat: *Amphimedon* sp.
Eng: Blue-finger Sponge
Deu: Blauer Finger-Schwamm
Size: up to 45cm high

Stingers

The comparably large group of stinging animals, scientifically known as Cnidarians, are exclusive to the watery realm and most species are marine. There are mobile and sessile forms. As for Huvadhoo, most of the cnidarians present are sessile corals belonging to a multitude of classes and families. To describe all of them would be to go way beyond the scope of this guide. The opposite holds true for mobile cnidarians. During the author's stay in the atoll, there was only a single species of mobile medusa observed: *Physalia utriculus*, the smaller relative of the deadly Portuguese Man of War. The much smaller Blue Bottle is venomous too but not deadly. However, their long stinging tentacles cause very painful injuries. But because these animals are comparatively seldom seen in Huvadhoo, I focus here on beautiful soft and fragile stony corals.

Soft coral

Lat: Octocorallia / Deu: Weichkorallen

Lat: Helioporidae – *Heliopora coerulea*
Eng: Blue Coral
Deu: Blaue Koralle
Size: up to 100cm

Soft corals are the colourful daubs of the coral reef and hence very popular with underwater photographers. Some people might think of these creatures as plants, however they are not. The free-living larvae settle and develop into a sessile, stinging filter feeder. In contrast to stony corals, soft corals do not incorporate zooxanthallae into their body tissues. Unfortunately, for some reason yet to be determined, these colourful varieties are not very abundant in Huvadhoo. Perhaps it is the weak current within the atoll that restricts them. The dive sites where you can find them all occur at the outer reefs, sometimes Hafsa Thila, and very small specimens can be seen under coral blocks at Mas Thila. On the inside of the atoll rather dull coloured Mushroom Leather and Broccoli Corals can be found on almost every island reef slope. The picture of the Magenta Soft Coral was taken at Hafsa Thila, the Orange and Yellow coloured ones at Nilandhoo Kandu on the east side. Mas Thila is also a very good place to see huge Smooth Sea Fans.

Lat: Alcyoniidae – *Sarcophyton* sp.
Eng: Mushroom Leather Coral
Deu: Pilz-Lederkoralle
Size: up to 50cm

Lat: Nephthidae – *Dendronephthya* sp. 1
Eng: Orange Soft Coral
Deu: Gelbe Bäumchen-Weichkoralle
Size: up to 35cm

Lat: Nephthidae – *Dendronephthya* sp. 2
Eng: Magenta Soft Coral
Deu: Magenta Bäumchen-Weichkoralle
Size: up to 55cm

Lat: Nidaliidae – *Chironephthya* sp.
Eng: Yellow Naked Soft Coral
Deu: Gelbhäutige Weichkoralle
Size: up to 30cm

Lat: Subergorgiidae – *Annella mollis*
Eng: Smooth Sea Fan
Deu: Riesenfächer
Size: up to 200cm

Lat: Nephthidae – *Litophyton arboreum*
Eng: Broccoli Coral
Deu: Brokkoli Koralle
Size: up to 80cm

Lat: Ellisellidae – *Ellisella* sp.
Eng: Cane Gorgonia
Deu: Binsen Gorgonie
Size: up to 70cm

Hexacorallia

Lat: Hexacorallia / Deu: Sechsstrahlige Blumentiere

Lat: *Cerianthus* sp.
Eng: Tube Anemone
Deu: Zylinderrose
Size: up to 35cm

Lat: *Heteractis aurora*
Eng: Beaded Anemone
Deu: Glasperlen-Anemone
Size: up to 50cm

The taxonomic order of Hexacorallia comprises more than 4,000 species that live all around the world. Their common characteristic feature is a six-fold symmetric larva during their early development. Sea anemones, black corals and stony corals are the most famous members. The first are home to the anemonefish. Certain species of black coral often host Penguin Wing Oysters. The oysters were once harvested in large numbers because they often contain pearls; approximately one in 60. But certainly the most important members of Hexacorallia are the stony corals. There would not be a single coral reef without them. Their aragonite skeletons are the base of all reefs and life associated with it (see hard coral for more detailed information).

Lat: *Amplexidiscus fenestrafer*
Eng: Balloon Corallimorph
Deu: Grosses Elefantenohr (Scheibenanemone)
Size: up to 30cm

Lat: *Stichopathes* sp.
Eng: Black Coral Whip
Deu: Drahtkoralle
Size: up to 150cm

Lat: *Zanthus* sp.
Eng: Encrusting Anemone
Deu: Krustenbildende Anemone
Size: varies with colony

Lat: *Heteractis magnifica*
Eng: Magnificent Sea Anemone
Deu: Prachtanemone
Size: up to 50cm

Hard or stony coral

Lat: Scleractinia / Deu: Steinkorallen

Without stony corals tropical reefs simply would not exist. They are the basis of all tropical coral reefs. Corals in a tropical reef act like trees in the rain forest. They are a life form themselves and yet so much more at the same time. Corals not only provide food and shelter. More importantly, they provide three-dimensional settlement space and thereby boost the habitat to produce the flourishing oases of biodiversity that we all admire and enjoy so much. Without corals, the tropical sea bottom would mostly be a sad, two-dimensional sand flat. Finally it is the corals themselves that support the entire tourism industry of the Maldives. The Maldivian archipelago is made of corals and hence without them, it simply would not exist.

It is their aragonite skeletons that build up reefs over millennia and keep the islands above the surface. Some branching species (e.g. Acroporidae) grow up to 15cm per year, while other massive species (e.g. Poritidae) grow only 3mm in the same time. This enormous yearly accrescence of matter is thanks

Lat: Acroporidae – *Acropora nasuta*
Eng: Nosey Coral
Deu: Nasen-Koralle
Size: up to 20cm

Lat: Acroporidae – *Acropora cervicornis*
Eng: Staghorn Coral
Deu: Geweihkoralle
Size: up to 100cm

Lat: Acroporidae – *Acropora palifera*
Eng: Column Staghorn Coral
Deu: Säulen-Geweihkoralle
Size: up to 70cm

Lat: Acroporidae – *Acropora hyacinthus*
Eng: Plate Coral
Deu: Hyazinthen-Tischkoralle
Size: up to 200cm

to the symbiosis between coral polyps and zooxanthallae algae, the so-called hermatypic corals.

Early on, it was thought that only a single species of zooxanthallae existed. Research over the last 40 years has found the exact opposite; there is in fact a stunning diversity. Together with the enormous importance of zooxanthallae, some scientists even argue whether it is actually the coral or rather the algae that supports all this life. After all, it is the incorporated algae that produce up to 90% of the coral's energy demands. In the end, it is the sunlight that provides the power for the entire ecosystem and that makes this story a success for the last 245 million years. Sunlight is also the reason why coral reefs only occur in the tropics, i.e. the waters between the tropics of Cancer and Capricorn. Only here occur the necessary conditions: clear water and temperatures between 20 to 30°C (although a few corals e.g. *Lobelia* spp. occur in temperate waters).

Unfortunately, temperatures can also rise above the tolerance limits of zooxanthallae. The effect is commonly known as coral bleaching. It already occurs if water temperatures exceed the annual average maximum by 1-2°C. Since the climate is changing on our planet, this happens more and more often, especially during El Niño conditions. There is good news too. The devastating bleaching events of 1998 and 2002 that wiped out stony corals in the northern atolls, did not affect Huvadhoo. The coral gardens of this atoll are still in a pristine state and the best places to see this for yourself are the dive sites of Coral City, Mas Thila and Wagaathu Gala.

Cnidaria   Chapter 3 — Identification guide

Lat: Poritidae – *Porites cylindrica*
Eng: Cylinder Coral
Deu: Zylinder-Koralle
Size: up to 100cm

Lat: Poritidae – *Porites rus*
Eng: Flame Coral
Deu: Flammen-Koralle
Size: up to 20cm

Lat: Poritidae – *Porites lobata*
Eng: Hump Coral
Deu: Grosse Porenkoralle
Size: up to 400cm

Chapter 3 — Identification guide   *Cnidaria*

Lat: Poritidae – *Porites* sp.
Eng: Blue Pore Coral
Deu: Blaue Poren-Koralle
Size: up to 120cm

Lat: Mussidae – *Symphyllia agaricia*
Eng: Brain Coral
Deu: Stachlige Faltenkoralle
Size: up to 35cm

Lat: Fungiidae – *Fungia fungites*
Eng: Common Mushroom Coral
Deu: Pilz-Koralle
Size: up to 20cm

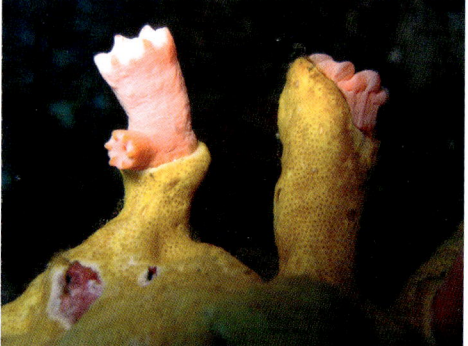

Lat: Dendrophylliidae – *Dendrophyllia gracilis*
Eng: Graceful Coral
Deu: Grazile Kelchkoralle
Size: single polyp - 3cm

Lat: Mussidae – *Lobophyllia hemprichii*
Eng: Hemprich's Brain Coral
Deu: Hemprichis Hirnkoralle
Size: streching over several meters

Lat: Dendrophylliidae – *Tubastrea micrantha*
Eng: Black Sun Coral
Deu: Schwarze Kelchkoralle
Size: up to 100cm

Cnidaria   Chapter 3 — Identification guide

Lat: Caryophylliidae – *Plerogyra sinuosa*
Eng: Sinuose Coral
Deu: Blasenkoralle
Size: up to 20cm

Lat: Dendrophylliidae – *Turbinaria reniformis*
Eng: Yellow Stony Coral
Deu: Gelbe Salatkoralle
Size: up to 150cm high

Coral reef ecology and conservation

When Charles Darwin first described coral reefs (1842) he had already stumbled across a most peculiar phenomenon that would later become known as the Darwin Paradox. He marvelled at the beauty and diversity of coral reefs just as much as we still do; however, he went a step further and asked the one question that still challenges marine ecological research today: "How can there be so much life in the middle of a deserted ocean, a nutrient poor habitat?"

This question is the essence of the Darwin Paradox and the answers provided so far are still not entirely satisfactory.

Coral reefs produce up to 10g of biological matter per square metre per day. This value is approximately 30 times above the so-called primary production value of the surrounding open ocean (0.34 g/m^2/day). One might assume that with such high production values coral reefs are almost inexhaustible sources of food and other resources; unfortunately, this is a fallacy and somewhat paradoxical. Let us call it the 'reef harvesting paradox'.

In contrast to other marine habitats, even with lower rates of production, coral reefs sustain only a very low harvesting level. "But how can that be, if there are so many fish?", you might well ask. The answer is poor nutrient availability. In order to cope with this situation, coral reef systems live in a permanent state of nutrient recycling. In fact, tropical rain forests face a very similar situation with regard to their very thin layer of topsoil.

Basically everything that is produced is consumed straight away again within the system. Scientists would speak of a low net primary production, i.e. the surplus that remains after all the fish and corals and other animals have breathed, reproduced and fed on each other.

You could compare the situation with a government that deducts taxes from the generated production (i.e. salaries, income, etc.) in order to sustain itself. However, you would never want to live in such a country, because the tax that coral reefs demand correspond to a tax level between 95 to 99% of income! Only the remaining 1-5% are actually harvestable without weakening the system.

Now imagine a subsistence fisherman facing this seemingly rich habitat with his hungry kids at home. Of course, it would be very difficult for him to understand the need for conservation, even if it is for his own good. As long as there is only a single fishing village, the resulting danger to the system is comparatively small and the fishing might continue for centuries.

However, our modern ways and times are changing this situation. Cities along the coast are growing rapidly as more and more people are choosing to move there. Accordingly, the stress on the ecosystem increases as the demand for food, as well as the pollution from sewage, increases. Demographers predict the coastal population will increase by 35% to 2.74 billion people in 2025, compared to 1995. By 2050, the world population will grow to 9 billion and the problem will hence worsen even further.

Under these circumstances, modern conservationists follow different strategies to cope with the ever-increasing stress to coral reefs. One of the most promising approaches is the creation of strategically well-placed Marine Protection Areas (MPA) and no-take zones. Their placement usually follows scientific recommendations, based on local research of marine current and larval distribution patterns in a way that protected areas support non-protected areas with fresh larvae and thereby refill depleted stocks. In theory, a well considered network of MPAs supports large areas with fresh larvae even at high levels of fishing pressure.

Another very successful strategy is the consideration of functional groups of species and their separate conservation and management. Taking special care of functionally important groups keeps the entire system alive by keeping up its capacity to repair itself and withstand disturbances. Scientifically, this ability is referred to as the system's resilience. The better the resilience, the better the habitat can withstand disturbances and stress.

A good example is the surgeonfish, which forage for algae that grow on corals and in doing so clean the surface of the corals so that these can continue with effective photosynthesis.

Softies – Molluscs

Lat: Mollusca / Deu: Weichtiere

Molluscs are the second largest phylum (i.e. a taxonomic order) after the arthropods, which comprise especially the insects. Estimates of described species range between 50,000 and 120,000. In the marine realm they make up almost a quarter of all species described to date, some 23%. Their diversity by means of shape, lifestyle, size and adaptation is unmatched. The group contains such unlikely relatives as octopuses, squid, bivalves and snails. They do have one thing in common though, a soft body. This is also where their name comes from, the Aristotelian notion of 'ta malakia', the soft ones. This guide only presents a few examples and common species of the area.

Bivalves

Lat: Bivalvia / Deu: Muscheln

Lat: *Pteria penguin*
Eng: Penguin Wing Oyster
Deu: Schwarze Flügelmuschel
Size: up to 25cm

Bivalves are usually sessile filter feeders. In the tropics, however, you will find an additional feeding mode. During their evolution, giant clams have incorporated symbiotic algae into their tissues and resemble corals in this respect. They still filter the water for food, but the importance of algae-derived sugars from photosynthesis increases with age. The algae of large clams produce more than 60% of their energy demands. Other bivalves like oysters have become famous for the pearls they produce. The Penguin Wing Oyster (on the picture overgrown by a sponge) was once harvested entirely with their hosting black coral bushes. The coral grows at depths of up to 40m and can host several oysters. The 'Valsalva' manoeuvre (nose pinching for pressure equalisation) was unknown to Maldivian pearl divers; they used to hit their head instead! This often led to bleeding noses, which in turn was regarded to be an initiation into manhood among pearl-divers.

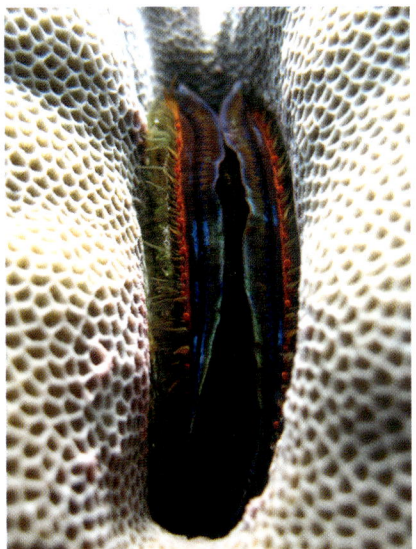

Lat: *Pedum spondyloidum*
Eng: Coral Clam
Deu: Irisierende Kammmuschel
Size: up to 5cm

Lat: *Chama lazerus*
Eng: Rough Cockle
Deu: Perlmuschel
Size: up to 6cm

Chapter 3 — Identification guide Mollusca

Lat: *Spondylus varius* / Eng: Variable Thorny Oyster / Deu: Stachelauster
Size: up to 20cm

Lat: *Hyotissa hyotis*
Eng: Honeycomb Oyster
Deu: Honigwabenauster
Size: up to 25cm

Lat: *Tridacna crocea*
Eng: Crocus Giant Clam
Deu: Eingewachsene Riesenmuschel
Size: up to 15cm

Lat: *Tridacna derasa*
Eng: Necklace Giant Clam
Deu: Glatte Riesenmuschel
Size: up to 50cm

Lat: *Tridacna squamosa*
Eng: Fluted Giant Clam
Deu: Schuppige Riesenmuschel
Size: up to 50cm

Univalves

Lat: Gastropoda / Deu: Schnecken

Univalves or Gastropods are commonly known as slugs and snails. Not all of them actually possess a shell, like some of the most beautiful species of nudibranchs. These species have become increasingly important in pharmacological investigations, as certain species contain natural toxins that serve as active ingredients in highly potent medicines. The odd looking Hiby's Lamellarid does have a shell, but it is overgrown by the mantel. The shells of cowries have long served an entirely different purpose. For hundreds of years they served as currency in parts of Africa, India and China. Later on, slave traders caused an inflation in Africa using Maldivian cowries. Don't worry though, they can still be found in the reefs of Huvadhoo. Please do not collect or buy them as souvenirs. Anyway customs won't be able to differentiate between those collected from the beach, the reef or bought ones that were illegally harvested.

Lat: *Tectus niloticus*
Eng: Common Turban Shell
Deu: Gewöhnliche Turbanschnecke
Size: up to 15cm

Chapter 3 — Identification guide   Mollusca

Lat: *Lambis lambis*
Eng: Common Spider Shell
Deu: Flügelschnecke
Size: up to 23cm

Lat: *Phyllidia elegans*
Eng: Elegant Phyllidia
Deu: Elegante Warzenschnecke
Size: up to 5cm

Lat: *Cypraea tigris*
Eng: Tiger Cowry
Deu: Tiger-Kaurie
Size: up to 13cm

Lat: *Phyllidia varicosa*
Eng: Varicose Phyllidia
Deu: Gift-Warzenschnecke
Size: up to 10cm

Lat: *Coriacella hibyae*
Eng: Hiby's Lamellarid
Deu: Malediven-Schwammschnecke
Size: up to 4cm

Lat: *Phyllidiella rosans*
Eng: Rose Phyllidiella
Deu: Rosa Warzenschnecke
Size: up to 3.5cm

Octopuses and squid

Lat: Octopodidae / Deu: Oktopusse

Octopuses are one of the most puzzling creatures on the planet. They change colour and shape within seconds, are very curious, very intelligent, communicate with conspecifics, and possess a diverse range of hunting strategies and defensive behaviours. Their intelligence is especially fascinating. The body holds nine brains, a central one and one in each tentacle. Experiments have demonstrated their ability to learn following observation. Their skin alone keeps scientists busy. It matches the colours and patterns of their environment, even though they are colour blind. When approached in the Huvadhoo area they usually turn red, which is why their common English name is rather misleading. Red colour is a sign of stress. Octopuses, like squid, also squirt ink when forced to flee. Sometimes the shape resembles the animal itself, a so-called pseudomorph. This causes some predators to attack the ink cloud instead of the animal which meanwhile escapes. It is called the 'Blanch-Ink-Jet Manoeuvre'. Snorkellers are especially advised to take their time and be patient when they have the chance to observe an octopus. It is best to stay calm and quiet on the surface for more than 10 minutes, sometimes longer. You will almost certainly be rewarded with a story to tell.

Squid, those magicians of the sea, are also sometimes found in Huvadhoo, as earlier mentioned (p.56).

Lat: *Octopus cyanea*
Eng: Big Blue Octopus
Deu: Roter Krake
Size: up to 80cm

Crustaceans

Lat: Crustacea / Deu: Krebse

Due to their strong exoskeletons, some people refer to this group of aquatic animals as the knights of the sea. The comparison is fair enough, though it somewhat disregards their immense diversity in terms of shape and appearance, as well as function. You could easily fill an entire book about crustaceans. Already the term 'crustacean' is a higher taxonomic order (subphylum) that comprises, among others, crabs, lobsters, shrimps and even sessile barnacles. Only four families are presented here.

The family of hermit crabs, Paguroidea, need additional armour but avoid long and dangerous periods of soft armour when moulting and instead just retreat into their homes (shells of gastropods). Naturally, hermit crabs also grow and consequently need bigger shells. In areas of low sea shell abundance this can lead to vigorously fought battles between hermit crabs.

Cleaner shrimps, Stenopodidea, are of a completely different nature. Apart from their long legs and antennae, they look pretty much like the more famous crustaceans, yet they fulfil an enormously important task in the ecosystem. As the common name suggests they clean other animals, mostly larger fish. Together with the cleaner wrasses, you could also call them the hygienic police of the reef. When approached carefully and offered a hand they might even clean your fingernails! You can find them waiting for customers in small caves.

Another lifestyle that completely diverges that other crustaceans is that of the genus *Alpheus* of the family of snapping shrimps, Alpheidae. Many species live in symbiosis with gobies. While the shrimp digs its common cavity into the sand, the goby stays on the watch and gives the sign for retreat in case of imminent danger as mentioned earlier (p.64).

Lobsters are especially well known as great eating. In the reef they can be found under larger coral blocks. In case you find one, don't tell your resorts chef or it might end up on your plate.

Lat: *Alpheus djiboutensis*
Eng: Djibouti Snapping Shrimp
Deu: Djibouti Knallkrebs
Size: up to 3cm

Lat: *Panulirus versicolor*
Eng: Painted Rock Lobster
Deu: Gestreifte Languste
Size: up to 40cm

Lat: *Dardanus lagopodes*
Eng: Hairy Red Hermit Crab
Deu: Blau Knie Einsiedler
Size: up to 5cm

Lat: *Stenopus hispidus*
Eng: Banded Boxer Shrimp
Deu: Gebänderte Scherengarnele
Size: up to 7cm

Lat: *Dardanus megistos*
Eng: Red Hermit Crab
Deu: Weißpunkt-Einsiedler
Size: up to 25cm

Spiny fellows – Echinoderms

Lat: Echinodermata / Deu: Stachelhäuter

Echinoderms are the most amazing creatures. Their diversity in terms of shape, appearance, habitat occurrence and function is not easily matched. This exclusively marine group of animals exhibits two main features: spines and a five-fold symmetry.

Their name derives from the ancient Greek word for hedgehog (Gr. echinos), which freely translates into spiny, and skin (Gr. derma). The spines can be extremely obvious as in sea urchins or almost invisible as in sea cucumbers, where they are reduced to tiny spikes on or even under their skin. Their five-fold symmetry is frequently neglected, especially in adult forms. In some five-legged sea star it is obvious, while some other sea star (e.g. Crown-of-thorns Sea Star) have many more arms. Sea cucumbers even feature two symmetries: bi-lateral, from front to rear, and penta-radial in terms of diameter. However, all echinoderms show five-fold symmetry at some stage of their development, some earlier, some later.

Sea lilies or feather stars

Lat: *Crinoidea* / Deu: Seelilien und Haarsterne

Almost all of the sessile sea lilies are restricted to the deep sea and are thus of no concern to this account, since they reside well beyond the depth limits of diving and snorkelling. Even professional free divers, who reach depths of more than 200m, will not see them. The species that we might encounter are the mobile feather stars. Opposite to their almost permanently attached relatives, they can crawl, roll and even swim. Along the reefs of Huvadhoo, they can be easily observed and are one of the most beautiful and elegant animals around.

Like all echinoderms, feather stars show the classical pentaradial symmetry. In some species this is quite obvious with their five arms, whereas it becomes more difficult with other species, which can have up to 200 arms. The arms serve the purpose of filter feeding; this explains the position of all their arms stretched out perpendicular to the current. These arms are very sticky and have a 'conveyor belt'-like functioning structure in the middle that transports food to the central mouth. Unlike other echinoderms, the intestines are U-shaped, thereby positioning the anus right next to the mouth. Many species though can extend the arms to deposit the debris away from the mouth. Just below the mouth you will find the cirri. These leg-like organs are either used to move or to hold on to various surfaces. Some species can even be found all the way out on the tip of sea whips. These normally nocturnal creatures can also occasionally be seen during the day, especially at Hafsa Thila in the west of the atoll. Many of the pictures shown here have been taken there.

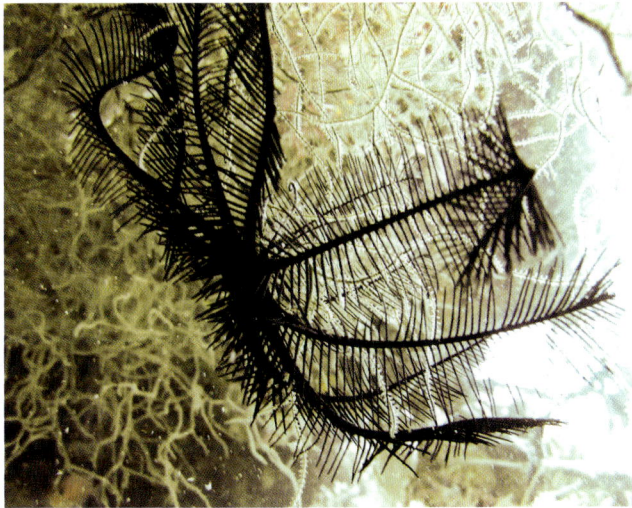

Lat: *Colobometra perspinosa*
Eng: Spinose Feather Star
Deu: Stachliger Haarstern
Size: up to 20cm

Lat: *Cenometra bella*
Eng: Pretty Feather Star
Deu: Hübscher Haarstern
Size: up to 14cm

Lat: *Himerometra robustipinna*
Eng: Robust Feather Star
Deu: Robuster Haarstern
Size: up to 30cm

Sea stars

Lat: Asteroidea / Deu: Seesterne

Huvadhoo offers an eclectic range of sea star species. Their sizes range from the small Indian Sea Star to large species like Guilding's Sea Star or the Crown-of-thorns. As earlier mentioned, the last also shows more arms than the classical five arms (pentamerism) of most of the others, or apparently no arms at all as with the Schmedelian Pincushion Sea Star. The Multi-pore Sea Star even appears to be one-armed at times. Of course this is not the case but rather the result of its common style of reproduction: budding. Many sea stars are actually capable of this form of asexual reproduction because all of their arms contain all vital organs. And a diffuse nervous system is favoured over a centralised one. All sea stars are predators. Many hunt bivalves that they open with their powerful arms, which also allow a slow but steady locomotion. One of the most vicious species is the Crown-of-thorns Sea Star that feeds on corals and can become a natural pest. Under certain environmental conditions and like the invasion of locusts in eastern Africa, they reproduce in vast numbers and can devastate entire reef systems. Since the beginning of climate change this regularly happens in southern areas of the world famous Great Barrier Reef in Australia.

Lat: *Fromia mileporella*
Eng: Thousand Pores Sea Star
Deu: Tausend Poren Seestern
Size: up to 5cm

Lat: *Fromia nodosa*
Eng: Noduled Sea Star
Deu: Knotiger Seestern
Size: up to 7cm

Lat: *Culcita schmedeliana*
Eng: Schmedelian Pincushion Sea Star
Deu: Indischer Kissen-Seestern
Size: up to 25cm

Lat: *Fromia indica*
Eng: Indian Sea Star
Deu: Indischer Seestern
Size: up to 5cm

Echinodermata Chapter 3 — Identification guide

Lat: *Linckia guldingi*
Eng: Guilding's Sea Star
Deu: Guildings Seestern
Size: up to 35cm

Lat: *Gomophia egyptiaca*
Eng: Egyptian Sea Star
Deu: Ägyptischer Seestern
Size: up to 20cm

Lat: *Choriaster granulatus*
Eng: Granulated Sea Star
Deu: Gekörnter Kissenstern
Size: up to 27cm

Chapter 3 — Identification guide Echinodermata

Lat: *Nardoa galatheae*
Eng: Galathea Sea Star
Deu: Galatheas Seestern
Size: up to 16cm

Lat: *Acanthaster planci*
Eng: Crown-of-thorns Sea Star
Deu: Dornenkrone
Size: up to 45cm

Lat: *Linckia multifora*
Eng: Multi-pore Sea Star
Deu: Kometenstern
Size: up to 10cm

Echinodermata *Chapter 3 — Identification guide*

Sea urchins

Lat: Echinoidea / Deu: Seeigel

Sea urchins are often regarded as sessile, venomous and dangerous animals. This is only true to a minor extent. They mostly feed on algal mats and consequently need to move about and are thereby only very dangerous to algae. Their reputation as being venomous to humans derives mostly from infected wounds caused after stepping upon them, not from actual toxins in the urchin itself. On the other hand, there are some venomous species too. Generally it is a good idea not to touch them, especially species with very thin spines such as the Banded Sea Urchin (see picture), but simply stay afloat. Be aware of your surroundings and admire their often stunning beauty when seen. This is actually quite difficult in the Huvadhoo area because most species hide deep inside the reef. Some even dig into the reef for protection (see Burrowing Sea Urchin). The Slate-pencil Sea Urchin is considered to be a living fossil, and is quite abundant in the reef around Hagedhoo island (dive site no. 19). When you go snorkelling there, just look into the cracks of larger coral blocks and marvel as to how these seemingly clumsy large animals got into them.

Lat: *Heterocentrotus mammillatus*
Eng: Slate-pencil Sea Urchin
Deu: Griffel-Seeigel
Size: up to 25cm

Lat: *Echinothrix calamaris*
Eng: Banded Sea Urchin
Deu: Bleistift-Diademseeigel
Size: up to 25cm

Lat: *Echinometra mathaei*
Eng: Mathae's Sea Urchin
Deu: Riffdachseeigel
Size: up to 8.5cm

Lat: *Echinostrephus molaris*
Eng: Burrowing Sea Urchin
Deu: Bohrseeigel
Size: up to 3cm

Echinodermata

Sea cucumbers

Lat: Holothuroidea/ Deu: Seegurken und Walzen

Sea cucumbers, despite their appearance, are actually the highest developed echinoderms. The classical pentamerism, which is almost invisible, can be seen when taking a cross section that will show the five lines of the ambulacral system. This very interesting channel system serves different purposes in echinoderms, including locomotion, food uptake, waste disposal and osmoregulation by means of pressure regulation. However, with sea cucumbers it is only used for movement. Many people think that these sluggish animals are just lying around all day, filtering what passes by in the water column. This is not entirely correct, depending on the species. Many of them are actually not moving much, like the Edible or Black Sea Cucumber. Species such as Graeffe's or the Spotted Sea Cucumber on the other hand move a lot when feeding. They use their tentacles to graze on algal beds. The author once observed a Royal Sea Cucumber rolling down the reef slope at a dizzying speed. It is questionable whether this happened intentionally or because it slipped.

Sea cucumbers feed on algae and detritus, organic residue lying on the ground, which is literally present everywhere. The afore mentioned Black Sea Cucumber is doing exactly that inside the lagoon, right in front of your beach bungalow, and can sometimes be seen there in large numbers. Some people wonder if this abundance is a sign of increased pollution. This is not necessarily the case, although it is likely to be a sign of increased food availability due to increased rates of sedimentation, originating, for instance, from recent construction work. Now with so many close to your feet, you will be prone to step on them. Don't worry, this is not dangerous to humans, though certainly painful for the cucumber but not lethal. However, it might be very dangerous for fish, due to the discharge of a soap-like toxin called holothurin, which can kill them at short range.

Lat: *Bohadschia graeffei*
Eng: Graeffe's Sea Cucumber
Deu: Graeffes Seewalze
Size: up to 25cm

Echinodermata

Lat: *Thelenota anax*
Eng: Royal Sea Cucumber
Deu: Riesen Seewalze
Size: up to 60cm

Lat: *Holothuria atra*
Eng: Black Sea Cucumber
Deu: Schwarze Seegurke
Size: up to 60cm

Lat: *Holothuria edulis*
Eng: Edible Sea Cucumber
Deu: Essbare Seegurke
Size: up to 25cm

Lat: *Synapta maculata*
Eng: Spotted Sea Cucumber
Deu: Wurmseegurke
Size: up to 200cm

Lat: *Thelenota ananas*
Eng: Pineapple Sea Cucumber
Deu: Ananas Seewalze
Size: up to 75cm

Lat: *Stichopus variegatus*
Eng: Varigated Sea Cucumber
Deu: Scheckige Seewalze
Size: up to 50cm

Chordates

Lat: Chordata / Deu: Chordatiere

The chordates are the highest developed group of animals and their common attribute is the so-called notochord. In some chordates this structure is present only for a short time during their early larval development and degenerates thereafter, as for instance in sea squirts. In the vertebrates, the notochord develops into a fully developed spine, including in divers and other fish. [Of course divers are not fish but both are vertebrates and hence related, at least from a biological point of view. Nevertheless, this guide will abstain from describing such comical species as for instance the 'Homo sapiens divemasteri' or 'Homo sapiens instructori'. They are anyway still comparably seldom found in the waters of Huvadhoo!] Rather, the focus here is placed on sea squirts, fish, sea turtles and dolphins. The fish section is further divided into two sub-sections, one on cartilaginous fishes, comprising sharks and rays, the other on bony fish, like moray eels and butterfly fish.

Sea squirts

Lat: Ascidiacea/ Deu: Seescheiden

You might have difficulties believing it, but these simply built animals are more closely related to you than they are to sea cucumbers. During their early development, sea squirt larvae show the first developmental step of a spine, the so-called notochord. They even have a rudimentary brain at this stage. However, later on both features degenerate when the larva settles and assumes its sessile lifestyle. Once settled, they start filtering sea water. Basically their body consists of a mouth, a stomach and an exhaust valve. Some species live in colonies and share a common exhaust valve, while others live alone (see picture of Smooth Ascidia). The species presented here are just a tiny collection compared with their abundance in the world's oceans. Worldwide, approximately 1,900 species have been described to date. Many of them are very colourful.

Lat: *Didemnum molle*
Eng: Soft Didemnum
Dou: Grüne Riffseescheide
Size: up to 2.5cm

Chordata – Ascidiacea   Chapter 3 — Identification guide

Lat: *Clavelina moluccensis*
Eng: Blue-spot Sea Squirt
Deu: Molukken-Keulenseescheide
Size: up to 1cm

Lat: *Ascidia glabra*
Eng: Smooth Ascidia
Deu: Glatte Seescheide
Size: up to 6cm

Shark biology
and the imminent need for conservation

Whenever people start talking about sharks the resulting discussion resembles an eclectic encyclopedia of myths, fears and half-truths which only shows that sharks suffer from a very poor 'press' and scientific outreach. In the best kind of situation, divers may be present who can contribute some of their shark adventures and who can thus shed some light on the actual biology of these largely misunderstood creatures. However, before one can understand the importance and problems of sharks and their conservation one must understand their biology.

First of all, sharks are fish but at the same time entirely different from other kinds of fishes, notably the main group of extant fishes, the teleosts or ray-finned fishes. Their skeleton is made up of cartilage, not bone. Their rate of reproduction is closer to cats than fish. As large cats do on land, sharks fill the ecological niche as apex predators. As such, they rightfully behave like the kings and queens of their kingdom, where humans will always only be tolerated guests.

Furthermore, in doing so, they fulfil an enormously important ecological function within their environment. Sharks are active hunters but, just as with any other living creature, they avoid wasting energy, which means they prefer easy prey. Easy in this context often means inexperienced, weak and sick animals. The selection and subsequent reduction of these animals from the environment is an essential function of nature, without which the gene pool of the concerned species would degenerate and, over the long run, become weakened to the point of possible extinction. Therefore sharks maintain the fitness of their prey; hence the most important principal of evolution: survival of the fittest. They are in effect the wolves, jackals and lions of the seas. This is true for the entire planet, as they have adapted to polar, temperate as well as tropical seas.

Having understood their importance in the environment, we can understand the need for their conservation. If the shark plays such an important role, why is their survival and conservation so difficult? As mentioned above, sharks have comparatively low rates of reproduction. Furthermore, they grow quite slowly and thus become sexually mature later in life. It takes some species fifteen years to reach sexual maturity. Most of the large shark species give birth to living offspring (viviparous) at a maximum rate of not more than 30 juveniles per year,

Chapter 3 — Identification guide

most species less. Egg laying sharks and rays do not exceed rates of 140 per year. These numbers are nothing in comparison to bony fish that reproduce at rates in the thousands and hundreds of thousands (although of course, suffer a very high mortality, both as juveniles and adults). While it is often enough to leave fish populations untouched for three to four years to make a full population recovery, shark populations need decades to fully recover.

Basically, politicians could introduce a fishery management that respects these last undeniable facts and all would be fine. Unfortunately, this is virtually impossible due to human greed and market demands. At a current estimated rate of 100 million sharks killed per year, sharks are likely to be at the brink of extinction within the next few years. The ecological effect of this decline and possible extinction on the world's marine ecosystems can only be guessed. Almost certainly, vast changes will be seen in the marine food web. Lacking the hunting pressure from above, the next higher trophic level of large bony fish would increase their populations and thereby increase the pressure on the next lower level. The resulting wave would spread throughout the entire system with results that can only be imagined, not estimated. Questions regarding the future evolution of involved species would be even further away from a sensible estimation. We are gambling with a system that is far too complex to be fully understood. We do know, however, that shark predation sustains, in part, the marine life on our planet, including many bird and animal populations, including human populations.

Next to this highly alarming and dangerous development, one has to point out the unbelievably cruel hunting methods that are used to catch sharks. The method of 'shark finning' involves cutting off the fins of live sharks and throwing the rest over board in order to save storage space for transport. The crippled sharks die slowly, or are eaten alive by smaller predators. Some people might even welcome this fate, thinking of sharks as cruel and vicious hunters of humans. This view is the result of unsubstantiated fear exacerbated by magazines, books and films and lobby work. On average there are no more than five deadly shark incidents annually, compared with 100 million finned sharks per year (Nb. most human attacks, which are generally the result of three main species (Bull, Tiger and Great White Sharks) occur in shallow cloudy water, near the beach or river estuaries, or against snorkellers who are seen from below and confused with the natural prey, e.g. seals or turtles. Many shoreline attacks occur at dusk and dawn when visibility is poor and humans are confused with the normal prey species). The cut-off fins are ultimately sold to restaurants and stores that resell them as shark-fin soup and are (highly erroneously) thought to be highly potent folk medicines in eastern Asian countries. The soup with the tasteless meat is also regarded as a highly prestigious symbol of social status and since the standards of these countries have constantly increased over the past decade, so has the demand for this symbol of wealth. Sold as medicine, the meat is believed to hold magical powers that, once eaten, are transferred to the consumer, supposedly in order to strengthen their health and sexual potency.

It would be unjust, unfair and incorrect to exclusively blame Asian countries for the ongoing slaughter of sharks for commercial reasons, even though they represent the largest market. Sharks are hunted all around the world and not only for their fins. Their teeth and jaws are used for jewellery and as souvenirs, their skin as leather for clothing, shoes and accessories, oils of their liver find their way into cosmetics like creams, lipsticks, hair dye and vitamin products and many others. Part of the problem is that these products are almost never properly labelled as containing shark, or parts and products of sharks.

The demand is satisfied by Mafia-like operating structures. Fishermen even enter marine protected areas, e.g. the Galapagos Islands off the coast of Ecuador, where they catch large and rare Hammerheads. The twist in the story comes from the fact that shark meat is actually poisonous to humans. It contains high concentrations of the toxin Monomethylmercury (MMHg) that can cause the opposite of the anticipated effects, i.e. reduced health and cause impotence. Unfortunately most consumers have no idea about this fact. Ironically, the MMHg actually originates from human pollution that is accumulated and transported through the food chain until the final link. The shark meat can contain very high and unhealthy concentrations above 4mg per kg versus the international threshold of 1mg per kg.

What can we do to counteract shark hunting? The best option is to simply not consume shark products in any form. Due to insufficient labelling we have to be informed consumers.

Chapter 3 — Identification guide

This list of fictitious names of actual shark products might help increase awareness:

English	Deutsch/German	Français/French	Italiano/Italian
flake, huss, rock salmon, rigg, sea ham, steakfish, grayfish, whitefish, cape steak	Seeaal, Schillerlocken, Kalbsfisch, Speckfisch, Karbonadenfisch, Königsaal, Steinlachs, Seestör	chiens, petite roussette, grande roussette, taupe, veau de mer	palombo, smeriglio, gattucci, spinaroli, cani spellati

Taken from: www.sharkproject.org

Nurse sharks

Lat: Ginglymostomatidae / Deu: Ammenhaie

There are three species of nurse sharks in the world. In Huvadhoo, just as in the rest of the Maldives, the Tawny Nurse Shark may be seen. Contrary to its larger and more aggressive Atlantic conspecific, it is famous for its docile behaviour. All nurse sharks are bottom dwellers and feed on a variety of invertebrates and smaller fish. However, Tawny Nurse Sharks are especially fond of octopus which they suck out of their reef hideouts by forcefully expanding their throats, which creates a powerful suction towards their mouth.

These animals also show a high degree of territorial behaviour whereupon they return to their usual resting places after a night's hunt. Here they can often be found in groups of between 10 to 20 animals stacked up one upon another, daydreaming.

Lat: *Nebrius ferrugineus*
Eng: Tawny Nurse Shark
Deu: Indopazifischer Ammenhai
Size: up to 320cm

Zebra sharks

Lat: Stegostomatidae / Deu: Zebrahaie

Zebra sharks are a rare sight during daytime dives. These animals are active during the night and thus the only chance to see them at daylight is during the early morning hours. Their awkwardly shaped bodies, together with their long and flexible caudal fin, makes them a very attractive sight for divers. Furthermore, zebra sharks are not known to be aggressive towards humans. They can usually be approached at close range when found dozing on the bottom during the daytime. Because of the stronger current, they are more often found sleeping on the bottom of channels, as the rapidly passing water eases their respiration.

Another reoccurring question about zebra sharks concerns where their name comes from, more especially considering the fact that their skin pattern rather looks like that of a leopard? The answer is simple: zebra shark juveniles (up to a length between 50-90cm) have a zebra-like striped skin pattern that slowly changes into the adult spotted pattern as they grow larger.

Lat: *Stegostoma fasciatum*
Eng: Zebra Shark
Deu: Zebrahai
Size: up to 250 cm

Chapter 3 — Identification guide   Chordata – Chondrichthyes – Cartilaginous fish

Whale sharks

Lat: Rhincodontidae / Deu: Walhaie

Without doubt, encountering a whale shark comprises the single most remarkable and impressive experiences in a diver's life. The moment when the gigantic animal passes by cannot be compared with anything else on this planet. Entirely confused by its size you wonder why you don't hear anything. Something as big as a three-storey building (up to 12m long) surely must make a sound. But no, not whale sharks; they simply pass by with mighty waves of their massive but elegant tail-fin. Without stopping, they move on like silent public transportation, with an armada of remoras as passengers.

    The best aspect of these gentle giants is their docility towards divers and snorkellers. The biggest danger emanates from the shark's sandpaper-like skin and their huge tail that is prone, on occasion, to knock out an unwary diver. In every other respect, Whale Sharks are entirely peaceful. Their large mouths are used only to actively suck in water that is pressed through their gills in order to sieve out plankton. The only place in Huvadhoo where a young Whale Shark was observed to date is Mas Thila in the West.

Lat: *Rincodon typus*
Eng: Whale Shark
Deu: Walhai
Size: up to 1200cm

Requiem sharks

Lat: Carcharhinidae / Deu: Requiem Haie

For many divers visiting the Maldives, sharks and other large fish are the prime reason for their trip. Fortunately, encounters with these unrivalled elegant animals are almost guaranteed. Along the island reefs within the atoll, you will most likely encounter the White-tip Reef-shark, whereas along the reef facing the oceans the Grey Reef-shark is common. Even though it is smaller, the latter resembles more what people imagine when asked to think of a classical shark, the brawny, muscular look of a powerful predator. The White-tip Reef-shark's head and torso is much flatter. The shape is an evolutionary adaptation to the preferred hunting grounds of reef cracks and crevices. However, both species frequent waters with strong currents where high plankton concentrations lure their preferred prey items, smaller fish. Speaking of hunting sharks, both species are absolutely harmless to divers. There are no fatal accidents with humans recorded for either species. Nevertheless, it is always a wise decision to treat them with respect for what they are — apex predators. As such, they do not fear any other animal, including humans, in their territory. Keep a healthy distance, don't touch them, remain calm and stay close to your group. The best chances to observe sharks in great numbers in Huvadhoo, especially Grey Reef-sharks, are provided at Nilandhoo Kandu during strong incoming currents and at Mareeha Kandu during weaker currents that cross the channel's mouth.

Lat: *Carcharhinus amblyrhynchos*
Eng: Grey Reef-shark
Deu: Grauer Riffhai
Size: up to 180cm

Chapter 3 — Identification guide   *Chordata – Chondrichthyes – Cartilaginous fish*

Lat: *Triaenodon obesus*
Eng: White-tip Reef-shark
Deu: Weissspitzen-Riffhai
Size: up to 210cm

Stingrays

Lat: Dasyatididae / Deu: Stechrochen

Stingrays, like sharks, belong to the class of cartilaginous fish, which means that their skeletons are made of cartilage rather than bone. These animals are quite common in the Huvadhoo area. Divers rather than snorkellers will see all species as they are normally found at the bottom of reef slopes. Sometimes stingrays also enter lagoons and can be seen there by snorkellers too. The Blotched Fantail Ray is by far the most common. The female is much bigger than the male and resembles an impressive flying carpet when hovering over the reef. The main characteristic feature is the sting, or barb, at the end of their tail. It is only used in defence and held over the head when threatened. Divers should stop their approach and slowly retreat when the tail is held up in this manner. Injuries caused by the stings usually only occur when swimmers and waders accidentally step on a ray that is half buried in the sand for camouflage. In many other places around the world these animals have been fed by hotel or dive shop personnel and can even be touched. This is not the case in Huvadhoo, where the animals are still wild and are not especially used to the presence of humans

Lat: *Taeniura meyeni*
Eng: Blotched Fantail Ray
Deu: Schwarzpunktrochen
Size: up to 180cm

Lat: *Pastinachus sephen*
Eng: Cowtail Stingray
Deu: Federschwanz-Stechrochen
Size: up to 180cm

Lat: *Urogymnus asperrimus*
Eng: Porcupine Ray
Deu: Igelrochen
Size: up to 100cm

Eagle rays

Lat: Myliobatidae / Deu: Adlerrochen

The family of Eagle Rays is not too large but includes some of the most beautiful and elegant animals on earth. Among them is also the world famous Manta Ray as they are regarded to be part of a subfamily of the Eagle Rays, the so-called Mobulinae. Unfortunately at this time, however, there are no Manta sites known within the Huvadhoo Atoll. Nevertheless, the smallest brother of the Manta Ray can be seen regularly, the Pygmy Devil Ray, *Mobula eregoodootenkee* (a medal to the person who can pronounce this name correctly). They only reach a minute 1.1m compared to their gigantic brothers, but they often swim in large groups of up to 15 animals. From January to April, i.e. during the north-east monsoon, Dheeva Giri is a great place to observe them.

The other much observed species of this area is the Spotted Eagle Ray. Just like the Pygmy Devil Ray, they often form groups (see picture). They are frequently spotted in areas with strong currents such as Nilandhoo Kandu at the atoll's east side.

Lat: *Aetobatus narinari*
Eng: Spotted Eagle Ray
Deu: Gefleckter Adlerrochen
Size: up to 350cm

Chapter 3 — Identification guide Chordata – Chondrichthyes – Cartilaginous fish

Group of Spotted Eagle Rays

Lat: *Mobula eregoodootenkee*
Eng: Pygmy Devil Ray
Deu: Zwerg-Teufelsrochen
Size: up to 110cm

Lat: *Manta birostris*
Eng: Manta Ray
Deu: Riesenmanta
Size: up to 760cm

Moray eels

Lat: Muraenidae / Deu: Muränen

Moray eels suffer from a bad image of being aggressive and malicious predators. This might even be true for their prey when they are hunting in the crevices of the reef, but certainly not for humans. We are far too big for them. The image probably derives from their snake-like appearance and constantly open mouth when encountered. This behaviour is neither threatening nor defensive, it actually assists respiration. Moray eels only have very small gill openings behind their head and lack solid gill covers. The solution is constant water pumping, achieved by opening and closing their mouth. Moray eels are predators and normally hunt fish during the night and sometimes they also feed on carrion. The notion that they are toxic is also false. The cause of inflamed wounds from moray eels is their bad dental hygiene. By the way, the smaller Black Cheek Moray, *Gymnothorax breedeni*, is far more aggressive than its much larger relative the Giant Moray, *Gymnothorax javanicus.* So be careful when you dive around the eastern corner of Hafsa Thila. You can certainly be bitten if you disturb one!

Lat: *Gymnothorax javanicus*
Eng: Giant Moray
Deu: Riesenmuräne
Size: up to 240cm

Chordata – Osteichthyes – Bony fish Chapter 3 — *Identification guide*

Lat: *Gymnothorax breedeni*
Eng: Black Cheek Moray
Deu: Breedens Muräne
Size: up to 65cm

Garden eels

Lat: Heterocongridae / Deu: Röhrenaale

Being extremely shy, garden eels are very difficult to approach. Normally divers can only observe their heads poking out of the sand into the current to feed on drifting plankton. They resemble fields of asparagus and are a highly reliable indicator of current direction. Look out for them on the sandy bottoms and slopes of reefs. In Huvadhoo they can be found at Leon's Giri within the atoll and generally on the sandy bottom of channels. The species depicted in the picture is likely to be *Heteroconger hassi*, common at depths between 15 and 40m. Other garden eels only live below 25m.

Lat: *Heteroconger hassi*
Eng: Garden Eel
Deu: Ohrfleck-Röhrenaal
Size: up to 40cm

Lizardfish

Lat: Synodontidae/ Deu: Eidechsenfische

Lizardfish are great to observe during snorkelling or diving alike. Moderately well camouflaged to the human eye, they usually sit on top of coral blocks or algae mats. They scan the water above for careless fish up to their own size. As soon as they spot a worthwhile piece of prey they leave their lookout in a split second and shoot at it. Sometimes this happens two or three times in a row and is very amusing to observe (unless you are the prey!). *Synodus variegatus*, the Variegated Lizardfish and most common species of this area, comes in colours from brownish to reddish grey.

Lat: *Synodus variegatus*
Eng: Variegated Lizardfish
Deu: Riff-Eidechsenfisch
Size: up to 25cm

Needlefish

Lat: Belonidae / Deu: Hornhechte

Needlefish are often observed in the open water between islands of the Maldives, as well as right on top of reefs where they hunt for small pelagic fish such as herrings. Larger individuals hunt alone, while juveniles often form great schools. In the Huvadhoo atoll, divers and snorkellers will mostly encounter the Crocodile Needlefish, *Tylosurus crocodilus*. The pictures below show a school of juveniles. The snout is comparatively large in relation to the rest of the body. They are preyed upon by larger pelagic hunters like tuna and visitors can often see entire schools jumping out of the water in an attempt to flee. When they are hunting, you will see another group of fish fleeing and jumping out of the water right in front of them.

Lat: *Tylosurus crocodilus*
Eng: Crocodile Needlefish
Deu: Krokodil-Hornhecht
Size: up to 130cm

Soldier- and squirrelfish

Lat: Holocentridae / Deu: Soldaten und Husarenfische

The species of this family are strictly nocturnal and are hence found only in caves and under coral during daytime. Their unusually big eyes are a clear sign of this lifestyle. They are also well camouflaged, as their red colour turns black during the night and in low light conditions at greater depths. The differences between the soldier- and squirrelfish is the spine that protrudes from the gill cover in squirrelfish and their relatively larger size (the Sabre Squirrelfish has a particular impressive spine). Furthermore, squirrelfish usually live alone and defend a territory, while soldierfish live and hunt in loose groups.

Lat: *Myripristis vittata*
Eng: Immaculate Soldierfish
Deu: Weißspitzen-Soldatenfisch
Size: up to 20cm

Lat: *Sargocentron diadema*
Eng: Crown Squirrelfish
Deu: Diadem-Husar
Size: up to 17cm

Lat: *Sargocentron spiniferum*
Eng: Sabre Squirrelfish
Deu: Riesenhusar
Size: up to 45cm

Lat: *Neoniphon sammara*
Eng: Spotfin Squirrelfish
Deu: Blutfleck-Husar
Size: up to 24cm

Pipefish

Lat: Syngnathidae / Deu: Seenadeln

Pipefish are in the family of the famous seahorses. In contrast to all other fish, in pipefish it is the male that becomes pregnant and incubates the offspring. During a rather long and elaborate courtship, the female places the eggs into the male's breeding pouch where they are fertilised and carried for about a month. After hatching, most species are minute copies of their parents and begin feeding on the same diet immediately. Their mouth is toothless; however, they possess a highly developed and effective sucking mechanism. Pipefish are very slow swimmers; most species rely on camouflage and are very rarely spotted. The species shown here is the most common in the Huvdahoo area, living in calm lagoons between algae-infested corals.

Lat: *Corythoichtys haematopterus*
Eng: Reef-top Pipefish
Deu: Liegende Seenadel
Size: up to 15cm

Trumpetfish

Lat: Aulostomidae / Deu: Trompetenfische

The family of trumpetfish is monogeneric and very small, consisting of only three species worldwide. *Aulostomus chinensis* lives in the Indo-Pacific. The female is grey in colour with a yellow caudal fin tip, while the male's body is entirely bright yellow. They are exclusively carnivorous and often approach their prey by mimicking floating debris. From within corals and other vertical features you can see them stalking their prey headfirst. They also use bigger fish, like groupers, to hide alongside and sneak up on smaller fish (see also Reef Symbioses page 66). A dirty trick for sure!

Lat: *Aulostomus chinensis*
Eng: Trumpetfish
Deu: Trompetenfisch
Size: up to 80cm

Cornetfish

Lat: Fistulariidae / Deu: Flötenfische

Cornetfish are a monotypic family with only four different species worldwide. In the Huvadhoo atoll you can find the Blue-spotted Cornetfish, *Fistularia commersonii*. Normally snorkellers and divers spot them at depths between 5 and 10m, either alone or in small groups. On the open side of the reef they hunt for smaller fish and small invertebrates. They have a limited camouflage capacity to adapt their colour to the surrounding environment. In combination with their elongated body and an assault style of attack, they become almost invisible to their prey. In Europe they have invaded the eastern Mediterranean via the Suez Canal and are now changing the regional ecosystem.

Lat: *Fistularia commersonii*
Eng: Blue-spotted Cornetfish
Deu: Flötenfisch
Size: up to 150cm

Lion- and scorpionfish

Lat: Scorpaenidae / Deu: Drachenköpfe

Lat: *Taenianotus triacanthus*
Eng: Paper Scorpionfish or Leaf fish
Deu: Großer Schaukelfisch
Size: up to 12cm

The scorpionfish represent one of the most fascinating family of fishes. The elegance of the lionfish is undisputed, while scorpionfish feature an impeccable camouflage. All species are toxic, but the poison only serves as their defence and is not used for hunting. Injuries to divers are normally self-inflicted due to carelessness. On the other hand, this is understandable given their camouflage. The stoic animals remain on the watch until it is too late for the diver. In the same manner they suck in passing fish. The picture of *Scorpaenopsis oxycephala* was made at Hafsa Thila, while pictures of lionfish are best taken during night dives. The Spotfin Lionfish can also be observed during snorkelling. You will find them at shallow depths of 5m under coral blocks.

Lat: *Pterois volitans*
Eng: Common Lionfish
Deu: Gewöhnlicher Feuerfisch
Size: up to 35cm

Lat: *Pterois antennata*
Eng: Spotfin Lionfish
Deu: Antennenfeuerfisch
Size: up to 20cm

Lat: *Scorpaenopsis oxycephala*
Eng: Smallscale or Tesseled Scorpionfish
Deu: Fransen-Drachenkopf
Size: up to 35cm

Sea bass

Lat: Serranidae/ Deu: Sägebarsche

The family of sea bass is very diverse and consists of many subfamilies and subgroups from which three are mentioned here: The big subfamily groupers, the subfamily basslets, and the soapfish tribe.

Soapfish

Lat: Grammistini / Deu: Seifenbarsche

Soapfish constitute a tribe that is very closely related to the sea bass subfamily of groupers. They are named after the toxic secretion from their skin which is released and foams like soap when the fish is stressed. The picture shows two rival specimens battling for dominance of the same territory. During the day the species is found under coral and in small caves (lower left corner of the picture). They are carnivorous and feed on crustaceans and smaller fish.

Lat: *Diploprion bifasciatum*
Eng: Yellow Soapfish
Deu: Zweistreifen-Seifenbarsch
Size: up to 25cm

Basslets

Lat: Anthiinae / Deu: Fahnenbarsche

"What do you actually call those small yellow fish that are whirling around the bigger coral blocks?" You often hear this question from interested visitors after they return from their first snorkelling trip. In most cases the species in question is *Pseudanthias squamipinnis*, the Orange Basslet. It may be difficult to believe but these beautiful little fish are closely related to the groupers. The dense schools, which can number up to a thousand individuals, are feeding on plankton. If you look closely you might find the yellow-reddish coloured males. They are born female, but when the last dominant male of the harem dies the next biggest fish will develop into a male. There are about 12 females per male. [Yes fellas, I know, life ain't fair!]

Lat: *Pseudanthias squamipinnis*
Eng: Orange Basslet
Deu: Juwelen-Fahnenbarsch
Size: up to 12 cm

Lat: *Pseudanthias evansi*
Eng: Yellow-tail Basslet
Deu: Gelbschwanz-Fahnenbarsch
Size: up to 10cm

Groupers

Lat: Epinephelinae / Deu: Zackenbarsche

Lat: *Plectropomus areolatus*
Eng: Squaretail Coral Grouper
Deu: Dunkelflossen-Forellenbarsch
Size: up to 50cm

Groupers are a very large family of piscivorous predators. The protruding lower jaw of the mouth that makes up almost a third of the fish is a characteristic feature. When opened during hunting it exerts an enormous drag on the prey that leaves the victim absolutely no chance of escaping. Some groupers grow up to 2m. The biggest species in the Huvadhoo area, the Black-saddle Coral Grouper, *Plectropomus laevis*, grows up to 1.2m. The species occurs in two colour variations, yellow-white-black and brown-white. Some sources argue that the yellow variety is actually the juvenile form. In the Huvadhoo atoll, both varieties may be of very different sizes, which rather points towards a sexual dimorphism.

Lat: *Gracila albomarginata*
Eng: White-square Grouper
Deu: Fenster-Zackenbarsch
Size: up to 45cm

Lat: *Anyperodon leocogrammicus* / Eng: White-lined Grouper / Deu: Spitzkopf-Zackenbarsch
Size: up to 50cm

Lat: *Variola louti*
Eng: Lunar-tailed Grouper
Deu: Mondsichel-Juwelenbarsch
Size: up to 80cm

Chordata – Osteichthyes – Bony fish   Chapter 3 — *Identification guide*

Lat: *Plectropomus laevis*
Eng: Black-saddle Coral Grouper
Deu: Sattel-Forellenbarsch
Size: up to 120cm

Lat: *Cephalopholis miniata*
Eng: Vermillion Rock Cod
Deu: Juwelen-Zackenbarsch
Size: up to 40cm

Lat: *Cephalopholis argus*
Eng: Peacock Rock Cod
Deu: Pfauen-Zackenbarsch
Size: up to 45cm

Chapter 3 — Identification guide *Chordata – Osteichthyes – Bony fish*

Lat: *Epinephelus caeruleopunctatus*
Eng: Small-spotted Grouper
Deu: Schneeflocken-Zackenbarsch
Size: up to 60cm

Lat: *Aethaloperca rogaa*
Eng: Red-flushed Grouper
Deu: Rotmaul-Zackenbarsch
Size: up to 70cm

Lat: *Epinephelus spilotoceps*
Eng: Foursaddle Grouper
Deu: Vierfleck-Wabenbarsch
Size: up to 35cm

Bigeyes

Lat: Priacanthidae / Deu: Großaugenbarsche

As can be seen from their large distinctive eyes, bigeyes are nocturnal hunters. Their large mouth indicates that they are carnivores. Family members are usually coloured bright red, which turns into pitch black during the night and at depth during the day. They can also have different colours. The common species of the Huvadhoo area is the Moontail Bullseye, *Priacanthus hamrur*, which can even change colour and pattern. They swim around in large schools at Haodi Galaa Giri.

Lat: *Priacanthus hamrur*
Eng: Moontail Bullseye
Deu: Indopazifischer Großaugenbarsch
Size: up to 40cm

Cardinalfish

Lat: Apogonidae / Deu: Kardinalsfische

During the day, divers can observe this nocturnal family under coral blocks. The smaller species often fill up the entire cave in dense swarms. During the night they come out to feed on plankton above the reef and larger species also hunt fish. For a change it is the female cardinalfish that have to court the males. In exchange the males take over the brood care by carrying the eggs in their mouths. This very interesting behaviour and lifestyle can also be observed in *Siphamia fuscolineata*, which lives as a commensal on the Crown-of-thorns Sea Star, *Acanthaster planci* (see also Reef Symbioses page 66).

Lat: *Archamia fucata*
Eng: Orangelined Cardinalfish
Deu: Orangestreifen-Kardinalbarsch
Size: up to 10cm

Lat: *Apogon leptacanthus*
Eng: Long-spine Cardinalfish
Deu: Fadenflossen-Kardinalbarsch
Size: up to 6cm

Lat: *Cheilodipterus artus*
Eng: Arrow-tooth Cardinalfish
Deu: Wolfskardinalbarsch
Size: up to 12cm

Lat: *Cheilodipterus macrodon*
Eng: Tiger Cardinalfish
Deu: Tiger-Kardinalbarsch
Size: up to 15cm

Lat: *Rhabdamia cypselura*
Eng: Swallowtail Cardinalfish
Deu: Schwalbenschwanz-Kardinalbarsch
Size: up to 6cm

Lat: *Siphamia fuscolineata*
Eng: Crown-of-thorns Cardinalfish
Deu: Dornenkronen-Kardinalbarsch
Size: up to 3cm

Lat: *Apogon apogonoides*
Eng: Plain Cardinalfish
Deu: Goldbauch-Kardinalbarsch
Size: up to 10cm

Chordata – Osteichthyes – Bony fish   Chapter 3 — Identification guide

Jacks and travellies

Lat: Carangidae / Deu: Stachelmakrelen

The family of Carangidae includes jacks, trevallies, pompanos and jack mackerels. Most species are very fast and enduring swimmers. They resemble tuna and even evolved some common characteristics by convergence, such as the finlets between the caudal and a second dorsal fin; however, they are not closely related. They hunt for small pelagic fish and crustaceans, which live in open water. In the Huvadhoo atoll, you will mostly encounter the Blue-fin Jack, *Caranx melampygus*. When you leave the inner atoll on a safari trip to the outer ring you might also encounter the elegant Rainbow Runners. These fish can form huge schools and will swim past your diving group in no time. Very impressive indeed!

Lat: *Trachinotus baillonii*
Eng: Black-spotted Pompano
Deu: Gabelschwanz-Makrele
Size: up to 55cm

Lat: *Elagatis bipinnulata*
Eng: Rainbow Runner
Deu: Regenbogen-Renner
Size: up to 120cm

Lat: *Carangoides ferdau*
Eng: Banded Trevally
Deu: Querstreifen-Makrele
Size: up to 70cm

Lat: *Caranx melampygus*
Eng: Blue-fin Jack
Deu: Pferdemakrele
Size: up to 70cm

Remoras

Lat: Echeneidae / Deu: Schiffshalter

Remoras are a rather entertaining fish for divers. Some are scared by them, mistaking them for small sharks, but they are absolutely harmless. Their first dorsal fin is modified into a suction disc that they use to hold on to larger marine animals such as sharks, turtles, mantas or dolphins. It is not quite clear whether this behaviour is an advantage, disadvantage or neither for the host. The relationship between smaller species that enter the gill cavities for cleaning and their large hosts might be of mutual benefit. In any case, the relation seems to be rather one-sided, whereby the remoras feed on the leftovers or faeces of their host and gain protection from their size. They might occasionally try to hitch a ride with divers. There are two possibilities, either let them do as they please and risk a love bite, or scare them away by trying to hit them. Just don't use your fins for you might end up back at the surface. If you allow them to become attached, they will loyally follow you to your boat, or even into ankle-deep water at the beach.

Lat: *Echeneis naucrates*
Eng: Slender Suckerfish
Deu: Gestreifter Schiffshalter
Size: up to 80cm

Snappers

Lat: Lutjanidae / Deu: Schnapper

Snappers belong to a diverse family with many school-forming small species and also some solitary large species. One of the most beautiful and abundant species is certainly the Blue-striped Snapper, *Lutjanus kasmira*. During the day, divers can observe the often immense schools lingering around coral blocks at depths between 15-20m. The larger specimens, such as *Lutjanus bohar*, can also be found on the menu at your resorts restaurant under the name: Red Snapper. Their firm meat is regarded by some as the best you can find in Maldivian waters.

Lat: *Macolor macularis*
Eng: Midnight Snapper
Deu: Gelbkopf-Schnapper
Size: up to 50cm

Lat: *Lutjanus kasmira*
Eng: Blue-striped Snapper
Deu: Blaustreifen Schnapper
Size: up to 35cm

Chordata – Osteichthyes – Bony fish *Chapter 3 — Identification guide*

Lat: *Lutjanus biguttatus*
Eng: Two-spot Snapper
Deu: Zweifleck-Schnapper
Size: up to 20cm

Lat: *Macolor niger*
Eng: Black Snapper
Deu: Schwarzweiß-Schnapper
Size: up to 60cm

Lat: *Lutjanus bohar*
Eng: Red Bass
Deu: Doppelfleck-Schnapper
Size: up to 80cm

Lat: *Lutjanus gibbus*
Eng: Humpback Snapper
Deu: Buckel-Schnapper
Size: up to 50cm

Fusiliers

Lat: Caesionidae / Deu: Füsiliere

Lat: *Caesio teres*
Eng: Yellow-and-blueback Fusilier
Deu: Blaugoldener Füsilier
Size: up to 30cm

Lat: *Caesio varilineata*
Eng: Thin-lined Fusilier
Deu: Vielstreifen-Füsilier
Size: up to 25cm

Fusiliers belong to the most abundant fish family in the Huvadhoo area and the Maldives in general. They can form gigantic schools, usually encountered at reefs exposed to strong currents. The moment when they circle you will be one of the most memorable experiences of your diving trips. Their sheer number is simply breathtaking. Fusiliers feed on plankton and will thus be found on the weather side of the reef, where the fresh plankton is accumulated by the waves. Although this side is naturally less comfortable for snorkellers, generally it is the plankton-rich side where you find more fish.

Lat: *Pterocaesio tile*
Eng: Dark-banded Fusilier
Deu: Neon-Füsilier
Size: up to 25cm

Lat: *Caesio xanthonota*
Eng: Yellow-back Fusilier
Deu: Gelbrücken-Füsilier
Size: up to 30cm

Lat: *Caesio lunaris*
Eng: Moon Fusilier
Deu: Himmelblauer Füsilier
Size: up to 30cm

Pursemouths

Lat: Gerreidae / Deu: Mojarras

Pursemouths are also called silverbellies, for obvious reasons. Snorkellers can usually find them inside the lagoon close to the reef edge right over the sand. Because of their silvery colour they are quite easily overlooked in sun flooded, shallow lagoons. They swim short distances and stop abruptly to look for food. They are not too shy and can be approached quite closely in these moments.

Lat: *Gerres acinaces*
Eng: Small-scale Pursemouth
Deu: Kleinbeschuppter Mojarra
Size: up to 25cm

Sweetlips

Lat: Haemulidae / Deu: Süßlippen

Their thick lips are the characteristic feature of this family and the reason for their other popular name: rubber lips. This feature also simplifies identification, especially for the completely differently coloured juveniles. An obvious example is provided by the Oriental Sweetlip, *Plectorhinchus vittatus*, and its offspring (see pictures). The adults of other family members are mostly only seen during the night and pictures of the Harlequin Sweetlip, *Plectorhinchus chaetodonoides*, during the day are rare. The juveniles of all species are active during the day.

Lat: *Plectorhinchus vittatus*
Eng: Oriental Sweetlip
Deu: Orient-Süßlippe
Size: up to 50cm

Oriental Sweetlip juvenile

Lat: *Plectorhinchus chaetodonoides*
Eng: Harlequin Sweetlip
Deu: Harlekin Süßlippe
Size: up to 60cm

Threadfin bream

Lat: Nemipteridae / Deu. Scheinschnapper

Threadfin bream are mostly found on the lagoon side of island reefs. They feed on invertebrates, crustaceans and other benthic (i.e. bottom dwelling) organisms. The most common species in the Huvadhoo area is the Two-lined Monocle Bream, *Scolopsis bilineata*. These fish are not too shy and can be easily approached. They are a good first motif for underwater photographers practicing on living objects.

Lat: *Scolopsis bilineata*
Eng: Two-lined Monocle Bream
Deu: Schärpen-Scheinschnapper
Size: up to 20cm

Emperors

Lat: Lethrinidae / Deu: Großkopf-Schnapper

Most emperors do not form swarms; more often you observe individuals that can grow up to 1m. They swim in the water columns in front of fringing reefs and occasionally hide between larger corals. The family is closely related to the snapper, which is usually quite a lot more noticeable. Both feed on small crustaceans and bottom-dwelling invertebrates.

Lat: *Gnathodentex aureolineatus*
Eng: Gold-spot Emperor
Deu: Goldfleck-Straßenkehrer
Size: up to 30cm

Lat: *Lethrinus obsoletus*
Eng: Orange-striped Emperor
Deu: Goldstreifen-Straßenkehrer
Size: up to 40cm

Lat: *Lethrinus erythracanthus*
Eng: Orange-spotted Emperor
Deu: Gelbflossen-Straßenkehrer
Size: up to 60cm

Chapter 3 — Identification guide   Chordata – Osteichthyes – Bony fish

Goatfish

Lat: Mullidae / Deu: Meerbarben

Goatfish are classic inhabitants of the sand flats in between corals. For the same reason you will often find them inside lagoons. They are easily identified by the two barbels below the lower jaw, which they use to find prey by excitedly grubbing through the sand. They stir up clouds of dust in this way and can be approached quite closely as they are almost entirely unaware of their surroundings (see picture of Dash-and-dot Goatfish). Most species live alone. The Yellow-stripe Goatfish is an exception and is usually seen in medium-sized schools over reef tops. The entirely yellow variety of the Yellow-saddle Goatfish is a speciality of the Maldives (picture shows both varieties).

Lat: *Mulloides vanicolensis*
Eng: Yellow-stripe Goatfish
Deu: Großschulen-Meerbarbe
Size: up to 32cm

Chordata – Osteichthyes – Bony fish Chapter 3 — Identification guide

Lat: *Parupeneus cyclostomus*
Eng: Yellow-saddle Goatfish
Deu: Gelbsattel-Meerbarbe
Size: up to 50cm

Lat: *Parupeneus barberinus*
Eng: Dash-and-dot Goatfish
Deu: Strichpunkt-Meerbarbe
Size: up to 40cm

Lat: *Parupeneus bifasciatus*
Eng: Double-bar Goatfish
Deu: Doppelband-Meerbarbe
Size: up to 35cm

Rudderfish

Lat: Kyphosidae / Deu: Ruder- oder Steuerbarsche

The species of rudderfish, also known as sea chubs that occur in the Huvadhoo area, live in large schools. They feed on algae. The Snubnose Rudderfish looks similar to rabbit fish, but they are not closely related.

Lat: *Kyphosus cinerascens*
Eng: Snubnose Rudderfish
Deu: Heller Ruderbarsch
Size: up to 45cm

Butterflyfish

Lat: Chaetodontidae / Deu: Falterfische

Butterflyfish are amongst the most conspicuous of all reef fish. Their bright colours and patterns are of an astonishing diversity. They are very popular with aquarium keepers and visitors alike. Every snorkeller and diver will quickly find their favourite fish among this family. The different species are readily identified by their patterns and colours. You could spend an entire holiday collecting their images. The 32 species recorded for the Maldives are easy to observe, even for snorkellers, because the majority live on the upper part of the reef. They mostly seek shelter and feed between corals, where they search for little crustaceans and plankton that grow and live on the coral branches.

Lat: *Hemitaurichthys zoster*
Eng: Black Pyramid Butterflyfish
Deu: Schwarzer Pyramiden-Falterfisch
Size: up to 17cm

Chapter 3 — Identification guide   Chordata – Osteichthyes – Bony fish

Lat: *Chaetodon falcula*
Eng: Double-saddle Butterflyfish
Deu: Keilfleck-Falterfisch
Size: up to 20cm

Lat: *Chaetodon kleinii*
Eng: Brown Butterflyfish
Deu: Kleins Falterfisch
Size: up to 13cm

Lat: *Chaetodon lunula*
Eng: Racoon Butterflyfish
Deu: Mondsichel-Falterfisch
Size: up to 20cm

Lat: *Chaetodon madagaskariensis*
Eng: Madagascar Butterflyfish
Deu: Madagaskar-Falterfisch
Size: up to 14cm

Lat: *Chaetodon ornatissimus*
Eng: Ornate Butterflyfish
Deu: Orangestreifen-Falterfisch
Size: up to 20cm

Lat: *Chaetodon trifasciatus*
Eng: Pinstriped Butterflyfish
Deu: Rippen-Falterfisch
Size: up to 15cm

Lat: *Chaetodon triangulum*
Eng: Triangular Butterflyfish
Deu: Indischer Baroness-Falterfisch
Size: up to 15cm

Lat: *Forcipiger flavissimus*
Eng: Long-nose Butterflyfish
Deu: Röhrenmaul-Pinzettfisch
Size: up to 22cm

Lat: *Chaetodon bennetti*
Eng: Eclipse Butterflyfish
Deu: Bennetts Falterfisch
Size: up to 18cm

Lat: *Chaetodon zanzibariensis*
Eng: Zanzibar Butterflyfish
Deu: Sansibar-Falterfisch
Size: up to 14cm

Chordata – Osteichthyes – Bony fish Chapter 3 — Identification guide

Lat: *Heniochus diphreutes*
Eng: Schooling Bannerfish
Deu: Schwarm-Wimpelfisch
Size: up to 20cm

Lat: *Heniochus pleurotaenia*
Eng: Phantom Bannerfish
Deu: Fantom-Wimpelfisch
Size: up to 20cm

Lat: *Chaetodon oxycephalus*
Eng: Pig-face Butterflyfish
Deu: Falscher Riesenfalter
Size: up to 25cm

Chapter 3 — Identification guide Chordata – Osteichthyes – Bony fish

Lat: *Chaetodon meyeri*
Eng: Meyer's Butterflyfish
Deu: Meyers Falterfisch
Size: up to 18cm

Lat: *Cheatodon auriga*
Eng: Threadfin Butterflyfish
Deu: Fähnchen-Falterfisch
Size: up to 20cm

Lat: *Chaetodon xanthocephalus*
Eng: Yellow-head Butterflyfish
Deu: Gelbkopf-Falterfisch
Size: up to 20cm

Angelfish

Lat: Pomacanthidae / Deu: Kaiserfische

Any snorkeller or diver will immediately recognise an angelfish, simply by their undeniable beauty. They have long been mistaken for butterflyfish; however, the spine that protrudes from their gill covers is a distinguishing characteristic the butterflyfish doesn't have. Some members of the family, like the Royal Angelfish, are specialists and feed only on sponges and sea squirts. Others have a more diverse diet, ranging from zooplankton to algae. In the Huvadhoo atoll two of the species shown here, the Emperor and Royal Angelfish, have only been observed next to the islands on the inside of the atoll. The other two, the Threespot and Yellowface Angelfish, were only found on the outside reefs.

Lat: *Apolemichthys trimaculatus*
Eng: Threespot Angelfish
Deu: Dreipunkt-Rauchkaiserfisch
Size: up to 25cm

Lat: *Pomacanthus imperator*
Eng: Emperor Angelfish
Deu: Imperator-Kaiserfisch
Size: up to 40cm

Lat: *Pygoplites diacanthus*
Eng: Royal Angelfish
Deu: Pfauen-Kaiserfisch
Size: up to 28cm

Lat: *Pomacanthus xanthometopon*
Eng: Yellowface Angelfish
Deu: Blaumasken-Kaiserfisch
Size: up to 40cm

Hawkfish

Lat: Cirrhitidae / Deu: Büschelbarsche oder Korallenwächter

Hawkfish are a real treat for beginners of underwater photography. Most species are sitting quietly on their coral branch and will allow the diver to get relatively close before they change position. Even if you chase them away, they won't go far. Hawkfish can provide numerous opportunities to take a good photograph and at the same time train you to approach a fish correctly, i.e. calmly and slowly. Most species in this area are solitary. They are born as females and some species live in harems. The largest female will change its sex if the dominant male dies. The name derives from their watching and hunting strategy. They feed on crustaceans and other planktonic animals that pass their territory.

Lat: *Paracirrhites forsteri*
Eng: Blackside Hawkfish
Deu: Forsters Büschelbarsch
Size: up to 22cm

Lat: *Cirrhitichthys oxycephalus*
Eng: Spotted Hawkfish
Deu: Gefleckter Korallenwächter
Size: up to 9cm

Lat: *Paracirrhites arcatus*
Eng: Ring-eye Hawkfish
Deu: Monokel-Büschelbarsch
Size: up to 14cm

Damselfish

Lat: Pomacentridae / Deu: Riffbarsche

The English name for the family Pomacentridae, damselfish, is misleading. The family comprises far more than only damsels. It includes the famous clownfish group, as well as humbugs, pullers and sergeants. Consequently the scientific evaluation of the exact taxonomic order is still in progress. The entire family consists of an estimated 360 species worldwide and more are likely to be found. Specimens of this family are the most abundant animals of the reef. Just as they are abundant, their colours, patterns and behaviours are diverse. Many juvenile forms look completely different to the adults and are often more attractive and thus more noticeable (see pictures). Most species are vigorous defenders of their territory. Some even grow their own algal gardens which they take care of and feed from. They will bravely attack any intruder and even divers are not safe from them, except anemonefish maybe. They first provocatively approach you then flee for shelter in their anemone. They all have one thing in common though; they are always a great pleasure to see in case of an otherwise disappointing dive.

Lat: *Amphiprion nigripes*
Eng: Blackfoot Anemonefish
Deu: Malediven Anemonenfisch
Size: up to 10cm

Lat: *Amphiprion clarkii*
Eng: Clark's Anemonefish
Deu: Clarks Anemonenfisch
Size: up to 14cm

Lat: *Dascyllus carneaus*
Eng: Indian Humbug
Deu: Indischer Preussenfisch
Size: up to 6cm

Lat: *Dascyllus aruanus*
Eng: Humbug Damsel
Deu: Dreibinden-Preussenfisch
Size: up to 8cm

Lat: *Chromis atripectoralis*
Eng: Blue-green Puller
Deu: Schwarzachsel-
Schwalbenschwänzchen
Size: up to 10cm

Lat: *Pomacentrus indicus* – juvenile
Eng: Indian Damsel
Deu: Indische Demoiselle
Size: up to 11cm

Chapter 3 — Identification guide Chordata – Osteichthyes – Bony fish

Lat: *Chromis ternatensis*
Eng: Swallow-tail Puller
Deu: Ternate-Schwalbenschwanz
Size: up to 10cm

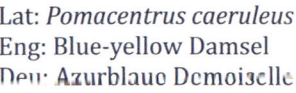

Lat: *Pomacentrus caeruleus*
Eng: Blue-yellow Damsel
Deu: Azurblaue Demoiselle
Size: up to 7cm

Lat: *Pomacentrus pavo*
Eng: Azure Damsel
Deu: Pfauen-Demoiselle
Size: up to 10cm

Chordata – Osteichthyes – Bony fish Chapter 3 — Identification guide

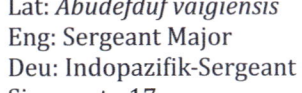

Lat: *Abudefduf vaigiensis*
Eng: Sergeant Major
Deu: Indopazifik-Sergeant
Size: up to 17cm

Lat: *Pomacentrus philippinus*
Eng: Philippine Damsel
Deu: Dunkelblaue Gelbschwanz-Demoiselle
Size: up to 10cm

Lat: *Chrysiptera brownriggii* – juvenile
Eng: Surge Damsel
Deu: Wellen-Demoiselle
Size: up to 8cm

Chapter 3 — Identification guide *Chordata – Osteichthyes – Bony fish*

Lat: *Amblyglyphidodon leucogaster*
Eng: White-breasted Sergeant
Deu: Weißbauch-Riffbarsch
Size: up to 12cm

Lat: *Chrysiptera unimaculata - juvenile*
Eng: One-spot Damsel
Deu: Einfleck-Demoiselle
Size: up to 8.5cm

Lat: *Plectroglyphidodon lacrymatus*
Eng: Jewel Damsel
Deu: Blaupunkt-Riffbarsch
Size: up to 10cm

Wrasses

Lat: Labridae / Deu: Lippfische

The wrasse family is the second largest family of marine fish after the gobies. Recent research also includes the parrotfish (listed separately in this book) with the wrasses, thereby increasing the number of species to more than 600. No dive or snorkelling tour in the Maldives will normally end without spotting some of these often very colourful fish. Additionally, many species exhibit distinct sexual and age colour differences, e.g. see Coral Hogfish. Their sizes range from the small but ecologically very important cleaner wrasse (~10cm), to the gigantic Napoleonfish (larger than 2m). A very characteristic feature is also their swimming style. Wrasses normally use only their pectoral fins for swimming while steering with the caudal fin. The bouncing movement reminds one of a butterfly. Most species are carnivores, feeding on other fish and sea creatures. It is not unusual to observe smaller species swimming alongside larger fish to get leftovers. They will also hunt for worms and other invertebrates. Larger species crack open bivalves, crustaceans or sea urchins. A highly specialised feeding strategy can be regularly observed from cleaner wrasses. They feed on the parasites that reside on the skin and gills of other, mostly larger, fish. They can even enter the mouth without being eaten. In this way, they contribute to the immensely important ecological function of reef hygiene.

Lat: *Labroides dimidiatus*
Eng: Blue-streak Cleaner Wrasse
Deu: Gewöhnlicher Putzerlippfisch
Size: up to 11cm

Chapter 3 — Identification guide　　　　Chordata – Osteichthyes – Bony fish

Checkerboard Wrasse juvenile

Lat: *Halichoeres hortulanus*
Eng: Checkerboard Wrasse
Deu: Schachbrett-Junker
Size: up to 25cm

Lat: *Labroides bicolor*
Eng: Two-colour Cleaner Wrasse
Deu: Zweifarb-Putzerlippfisch
Size: up to 14cm

Lat: *Gomphosus caeruleus*
Eng: Bird Wrasse
Deu: Vogel-Lippfisch
Size: up to 25cm

Lat: *Hemigymnus melapterus*
Eng: Half-and-Half Wrasse
Deu: Zweifarben-Bannerlippfisch
Size: up to 50cm

Half-and-Half Wrasse juvenile

Lat: *Cheilinus fasciatus*
Eng: Banded Maori Wrasse
Deu: Rotbrust-Prachtlippfisch
Size: up to 38cm

Lat: *Thalassoma hardwicke*
Eng: Six-bar Wrasse
Deu: Hardwickes Junker
Size: up to 20cm

Chapter 3 — Identification guide Chordata – Osteichthyes – Bony fish

Lat: *Cheilinus undulatus*
Eng: Napoleon Fish
Deu: Napoleon
Size: up to 200cm

Lat: *Bodianus axillaris*
Eng: Coral Hogfish
Deu: Zweifleck-Schweinslippfisch
Size: up to 20cm

Coral Hogfish juvenile

Lat: *Cheilinus trilobatus*
Eng: Triple-tail Maori Wrasse
Deu: Dreizack-Prachtlippfisch
Size: up to 40cm

Parrotfish

Lat: Scaridae / Deu: Papageifische

Parrotfish belong to the wrasse family. However, due to their immense importance for the functioning of reefs they are described separately here. Many parrotfish regularly feed on the algae that grow on corals, or even exclusively on the coral polyps. Accordingly, their teeth have grown together to form the necessary scraping plates. Snorkellers and divers alike can hear them feeding during visits to the reef. The result of their ongoing efforts is the bright white sand that is discharged in long raining trails and that we all love so much when we are lying on our towels in the sun. The production of this sand keeps the process of coral reef and tropical island formation alive. Not only does the fulfilment of this vital ecological function make these fish so interesting, they also have some unique traits. Some species wrap themselves in mucus during the night, an action that is thought to suppress their smell from potential predators. Furthermore, parrotfish show different colour patterns during different life phases (see pictures). For this reason the group of parrotfish was long thought to be much larger than it actually is, around 300 species instead of only 80.

Lat: *Cetoscarus bicolor*
Eng: Two-colour Parrotfish
Deu: Masken-Papageifisch
Size: up to 90cm

Two-colour Parrotfish juvenile

Lat: *Scarus strongylocephalus*
Eng: Sheephead Parrotfish
Deu: Indischer Buckelkopf
Size: up to 70cm
left female, right male

Lat: *Scarus sordidus*
Eng: Bullethead Parrotfish
Deu: Kugelkopf-Papageifisch
Size: up to 40cm
left male, right female

Lat: *Scarus prasiognathus*
Eng: Green-face Parrotfish
Deu: Singapur-Papageifisch
Size: up to 60cm
left male, right female

Sandperch

Lat: Pinguipedidae / Deu: Sandbarsche

Sandperch look similar to lizardfish but they are not closely related. On the other hand, they do share the same hunting strategy, staying on guard and attacking any smaller fish or crustaceans passing by. Unlike lizardfish, however, you do not find them sitting on coral too often but rather on sand, mostly under the coral blocks in the Huvadhoo area (see picture). Hirifushi Faru and Leon's Giri are good places to spot them.

Lat: *Parapercis millipunctata*
Eng: Black-dotted Sandperch
Deu: Vielpunkt-Sandbarsch
Size: up to 15cm

Lat: *Parapercis hexophthalama*
Eng: Speckled Sandperch
Deu: Schwanzfleck-Sandbarsch
Size: up to 25cm

Blennies

Lat: Blenniidae / Deu: Schleimfische

The family of blennies consists of around 350 species. Just like gobies, they don't have a swim bladder, which is the reason for their close association with the reef. Many species hide in small cracks and crevices, retreating into them when threatened. In order to be able to look out, some species swim backwards into the cracks, like parking a car, e.g. Two-colour Combtooth Blenny. Their name actually derives from the Greek word 'blennos', which means slime and refers to the thick layer around their bodies that serves as protection from being eaten. They feed on different types of food but mostly on zooplankton. Some blennies imitate other fish (mimicry) to either improve hunting or protection, e.g. the Imposter Blenny imitates Smith's Venomous Blenny. The latter is toxic and will bite predators in their gums so as to make them spit them out again.

Lat: *Meiacanthus smithi*
Eng: Smith's Venomous Blenny
Deu: Malediven-Säbelzahn-Schleimfisch
Size: up to 7.5cm

Lat: *Plagiotremus rhinorhynchos*
Eng: Tube-worm Blenny (upper fish)
Deu: Blaustreifen-Säbelzahn-Schleimfisch
Size: up to 12cm

Lat: *Plagiotremus phenax*
Eng: Imposter Blenny
Deu: Aggressiver Säbelzahn-Schleimfisch
Size: up to 5cm

Chordata – Osteichthyes – Bony fish   Chapter 3 — Identification guide

Lat: *Petroscirtes mitratus*
Eng: Crested Sabretooth Blenny
Deu: Segelflossen-Säbelzahn-Schleimfisch
Size: up to 6.5cm

Lat: *Ecsenius minutus*
Eng: Little Combtooth Blenny
Deu: Halsband-Wippschwimmer
Size: up to 5cm

Lat: *Ecsenius lineatus*
Eng: Lined Combtooth Blenny
Deu: Längsstreifen-Wippschwimmer
Size: up to 10cm

Lat: *Ecsenius bicolor*
Eng: Two-colour Combtooth Blenny
Deu: Zweifarben-Wippschwimmer
Size: up to 8.5cm

Lat: *Blenniella chrysospilos*
Eng: Orange-spotted Blenny
Deu: Blutstropfen-Felshüpfer
Size: up to 12cm

Triplefins

Lat: Tripterygiidae / Deu: Dreiflossen-Schleimfische

Triplefins, a large family with many species (>150), are rarely seen in the Maldives. This is due in part to their small size and because they prefer to live hidden away inside caves. Not many species have been seen here. Reports total up to not more than ten records for the entire archipelago. The family can be distinguished from the closely related blennies and gobies by three dorsal fins. The local species, *Helcogramma maldivensis*, can also be found around Sri Lanka. They feed on plankton.

Lat: *Helcogramma maldivensis*
Eng: Maldives Triplefin
Deu: Maledivischer Dreiflossen-Schleimfisch
Size: up to 4cm

Gobies

Lat: Gobiidae / Deu: Grundeln

The gobies are the largest family of marine fish with more than 2,000 species, and new species are regularly discovered. Gobies live all around the world, from the poles to the tropics, in salty and fresh water. One of the secrets of their success is their enormous diversity of lifestyles, or adaptability in an evolutionary sense. Gobies are benthic, that is bottom inhabiting animals, but they are not restricted to the bottom of the sea. They live just as successfully on corals, underneath the sand, on the bottom in symbiosis with shrimps (e.g. Crocus Shrimp Goby), on thin sea whips high above the bottom (e.g. Whip Goby), inside of giant clams or amongst the branches of Staghorn Corals (e.g. Yellow Coral-goby). Their food sources are equally diverse, some filter sand (e.g. Six-spot Sleeper-goby), others hunt for plankton or crustaceans. They can be beautiful like the Red Fire-goby, or inconspicuous and adapted to the sand like the Six-spot Sleeper-goby. They live at all depths and therefore can be just as well observed by snorkellers as by divers. It is speculated that there are hundreds more species yet to be discovered, so it is probably a good idea to grab your mask and fins and find them. Don't forget your camera!

Lat: *Ctenogobiops crocineus*
Eng: Crocus Shrimp Goby
Deu: Goldstreifen-Grundel
Size: up to 7.5cm

Chapter 3 — Identification guide   Chordata – Osteichthyes – Bony fish

Lat: *Valenciennea sexguttata*
Eng: Six-spot Sleeper-goby
Deu: Blaupunkt-Schläfergrundel
Size: up to 16cm

Lat: *Fusigobius* sp.
Eng: Orange-spotted Sand-goby
Deu: Orangepunkt-Grundel
Size: up to 7cm

Lat: *Brianinops* sp.
Eng: Whip Goby
Deu: Seepeitschen Grundel
Size: up to 2cm

Lat: *Gobiodon citrinus*
Eng: Yellow Coral-goby
Deu: Zitronengrundel
Size: up to 6.5cm

Lat: *Nemateleotris magnifica*
Eng: Red Fire-goby
Deu: Pracht-Schwertgrundel
Size: up to 7cm

Lat: *Amblygobius semicinctus*
Eng: White-barred Reef-goby
Deu: Weißband-Schläfergrundel
Size: up to 10cm

Lat: *Amblygobius hectori*
Eng: Hector's Reef-goby
Deu: Hector Grundel
Size: up to 6.5cm

Chapter 3 — Identification guide Chordata – Osteichthyes – Bony fish

Batfish

Lat: Ephippidae / Deu: Fledermausfische

Juvenile Batfish

Batfish are one of the all time favourites among divers. This is certainly due to their conspicuous shape but more likely because of their curiosity. There are many reports of batfish that have followed divers. The author himself was once followed by a fully-grown couple during half of a dive. The species grows up to half a metre and is very impressive with its large fins. The juveniles are especially attractive with their even greater fin to body ratio. Batfish feed on algae and small invertebrates but have also been observed feeding on jellyfish.

Lat: *Platax orbicularis*
Eng: Rounded Batfish
Deu: Rundkopf-Fledermausfisch
Size: up to 50cm

Chordata – Osteichthyes – Bony fish Chapter 3 — *Identification guide*

Rabbitfish

Lat: Siganidae / Deu: Kaninchenfische

The rabbitfish family is also monogeneric. It consists of only the single genus *Siganus* with 26 species. All of them feed exclusively on algae. Their name is supposed to originate from their nibbling way of feeding and the fact that they are quite shy and flighty. The spines of the dorsal fin are toxic. The poison is not deadly for humans but it can cause severe pain.

Lat: *Siganus stellatus*
Eng: Starry Rabbitfish
Deu: Tüpfel-Kaninchenfisch
Size: up to 40cm

Lat: *Siganus guttatus*
Eng: Sri Lankan Rabbitfish
Deu: Goldfleck-Kaninchenfisch
Size: up to 40cm

Lat: *Siganus puelloides*
Eng: Chin-strap Rabbitfish
Deu: Traueraugen-Kaninchenfisch
Size: up to 30cm

Moorish idols

Lat: Zanclidae / Deu: Halfterfische

The family of moorish idols is monotypic, which means that the entire family consists of only a single species, the Moorish Idol, *Zanclus cornutus*. The fish is very common in the Huvadhoo area and occurs mostly singly or in pairs, but rarely in small groups. Along the African coast, the fish is believed to be a sign of happiness and indeed it makes one happy to watch this beautiful creature. The species feeds on algae, sponges, bryozoans and other sessile species. They look similar to two species of butterflyfish in the area, *Heniochus diphreutes* (see also Butterflyfish page 153) and *H. acuminatus*.

Lat: *Zanclus cornutus*
Eng: Moorish Idol
Deu: Halterfisch
Size: up to 22cm

Surgeonfish

Lat: Acanthuridae / Deu: Doktorfische

Surgeonfish can easily be identified by the 'scalpel' at the end of their body in front of the caudal fin. For many species there is a single blade per side. During normal swimming, only the back is visible as the blade is only exposed when the fish bends its tail (Acanthurinae). There are also species with two and more blades that are permanently exposed (Prionurinae). The elegant Orange-spine Unicornfish for example possess two bright spines on each side that cannot be retracted. These heavily modified scales do not serve any hunting purpose, as had been thought for many years, but are of a purely defensive nature. Most species of surgeonfish feed on algae anyway. Some species, like the Convict Surgeonfish, form feeding schools when food becomes scarce (see picture). This way they can enter occupied territories more easily. By feeding on algal, surgeonfish fulfil a very important ecological function as they remove algal growth from sunlight dependant corals.

Lat: *Acanthurus triostegus*
Eng: Convict Surgeonfish
Deu: Gitter-Doktorfisch
Size: up to 22cm

Lat: *Acanthurus lineatus*
Eng: Lined Surgeonfish
Deu: Blaustreifen-Doktorfisch
Size: up to 35cm

Lat: *Acanthurus mata*
Eng: Pale Surgeonfish
Deu: Schwarzdorn-Doktorfisch
Size: up to 45cm

Lat: *Acanthurus leucosternon*
Eng: Powder-blue Surgeonfish
Deu: Weißkehl-Doktorfisch
Size: up to 22cm

Lat: *Ctenochtaetus strigosus*
Eng: Gold-ring Bristletooth
Deu: Goldring-Borstenzahndoktor
Size: up to 18cm

Lat: *Ctenochtaetus striatus*
Eng: Fine-lined Bristletooth
Deu: Längsstreifen-Doktorfisch
Size: up to 26cm

Lat: *Naso brevirostris*
Eng: Spotted Unicornfish
Deu: Langnasendoktor
Size: up to 55cm

Chordata – Osteichthyes – Bony fish   Chapter 3 — Identification guide

Lat: *Naso lituratus*
Eng: Orange-spine Unicornfish
Deu: Gelbklingen-Nasendoktor
Size: up to 45cm

Lat: *Naso hexacanthus*
Eng: Sleek Unicornfish
Deu: Blauklingen-Nasendoktor
Size: up to 75cm

Barracudas

Lat: Sphyraenidae / Deu: Barrakudas

Barracudas are a group of large marine predators. Just like sharks, they have a reputation for being especially vicious and dangerous, but as with their cartilaginous counterparts, this image is based largely on excessive exaggeration, rare accidents and rumours. However, there does exist a twofold danger. These fish are known to be attracted to and attack shiny objects such as silvery rings, as these may be mistaken for prey. The other danger lies in the consumption of their flesh. Because barracudas are at the top of the food chain they accumulate a toxin called ciguatoxin, a potentially harmful neurotoxin.

Barracudas occur in large shoals when they are young but become loners as they grow. These large mavericks are especially scary when they watch you with a penetrating stare while you take your three minutes safety stop on 5m. Just make sure you cover the shining parts of your equipment. In every other respect, barracudas are fascinating, elegant animals, and encounters with large shoals are often among the most memorable experiences of the holiday.

Lat: *Sphyraena barracuda*
Eng: Great Barracuda
Deu: Großer Barrakuda
Size: up to 200cm

Chordata – Osteichthyes – Bony fish *Chapter 3 — Identification guide*

Mackerels and tuna

Lat: Scombridae / Deu: Makrelen und Thunfische

There are many different tuna in the Huvadhoo atoll but only the Dogtooth Tuna can be found regularly. Larger species can easily be found on the menu of your resort's restaurant and will certainly be from the area. Tuna belong to the main food items of the local Maldivian kitchen. They live on the high seas and their entire body speaks the language of speed. The lateral line of the local species is curled (see picture), thereby following the direction of water turbulence when swimming at high speeds. They feed on smaller fish like fusiliers and grow up to 2m long and 30kg in weight.

Lat: *Gymnosarda unicolor*
Eng: Dogtooth Tuna
Deu: Hundezahn-Thunfisch
Size: up to 200cm

Lefteye flounder

Lat: Bothidae / Deu: Linksaugen-Flundern

Adult flounders have evolved to lie on their sides, so what we see is not their back but one of their sides. The lefteye flounders choose the left side to be at the top. They live well camouflaged on the sand of shallow lagoons and reef slopes. In the Huvadhoo region, the Leopard Flounder can be found in the rather silty sands of harbours, where they search for bottom-dwelling smaller fish and other invertebrates.

Lat: *Bothus pantherinus*
Eng: Leopard Flounder
Deu: Pantherbutt
Size: up to 30cm

Boxfish

Lat: Ostrociidae / Deu: Kofferfische

Boxfish are rarely seen in the Huvadhoo atoll, a fact possibly explained by their tendency to hide under corals. Their scales have fused and form a solid boxlike carapax, leaving only holes for the fins. The construction makes them poor swimmers but also protects them from most predators. Together with the hiding behaviour this helps them to survive. The picture shows a fully-grown male Yellow Boxfish, *Ostracion cubicus*. The females are smaller and often pale yellow in colour, while the juveniles are bright yellow with black dots and are more roundly shaped than rectangular. The car manufacturer Mercedes Benz based one of their concept vehicle designs on the shape of *O. cubicus* and found the aerodynamics to be very efficient.

Lat: *Ostracion cubicus*
Eng: Yellow Boxfish
Deu: Gelbbrauner-Kofferfisch
Size: up to 45 cm

Triggerfish

Lat: Balistidae / Deu: Drückerfische

Triggerfish are a very beautiful, although shy, family of fish. Their first dorsal spine can be erected and locked by the second spine. This mechanism serves as a security measure during the night to tightly lock them into reef cracks. Predators will have difficulties trying to prise them out. Throughout the Maldives, where the Blue Triggerfish is a very common sight, it can only be seen in small numbers on the outer reefs of the Huvadhoo atoll. Just as uncommon for the Maldives are the peaceful Giant Triggerfish that have been known to attack careless divers in order to protect their clutch. So far no attacks have been reported from the Huvadhoo atoll.

Lat: *Balistapus undulatus*
Eng: Striped Triggerfish
Deu: Gelbschwanz-Drücker
Size: up to 30cm

Chordata – Osteichthyes – Bony fish   Chapter 3 — Identification guide

Lat: *Balistoides conspicillum*
Eng: Clown Triggerfish
Deu: Leoparden-Drückerfisch
Size: up to 35cm

Lat: *Odonus niger*
Eng: Blue Triggerfish
Deu: Rotzahn-Drückerfisch
Size: up to 40cm

Lat: *Sufflamen bursa*
Eng: Boomerang Triggerfish
Deu: Blasser Drückerfisch
Size: up to 20cm

Lat: *Sufflamen chrysopterus*
Eng: Half-moon Triggerfish
Deu: Halbmond-Drückerfisch
Size: up to 20cm

Lat: *Balistoides viridescens*
Eng: Giant or Titan Triggerfish
Deu: Riesen-Drückerfisch
Size: up to 75cm

Filefish

Lat: Monacanthidae / Deu: Feilenfische

These rather odd looking fish are closely related to the triggerfish, which becomes apparent when looking at the first dorsal spines. Their name is meant to derive from their rough skin; stories tell that they were once used to polish wooden boat hulls. In this area there are two species which are moderately common, the biggest filefish of the family, the Scrawled Filefish, *Aluterus scriptus*, and its much smaller relative the Long-nose Filefish, *Oxymonacanthus longirostris*. The latter feeds exclusively on coral polyps, while its larger relative feeds on a diverse diet of algae, seagrass and small benthic invertebrates. They have also been observed to feed on jellyfish. Neither of the two species are good swimmers, which leads both to have evolved concealment behaviour. This is no problem for the Long-nose Filefish but you will laugh when observing its 1m long relative desperately trying to hide from you under a small table coral.

Lat: *Oxymonacanthus longirostris*
Eng: Long-nose Filefish
Deu: Palettenstachler
Size: up to 10cm

Lat: *Aluterus scriptus*
Eng: Scrawled Filefish
Deu: Schrift-Feilenfisch
Size: up to 100cm

Pufferfish

Lat: Tetraodontidae / Deu: Kugelfische

Pufferfish are amongst the most poisonous fish on the planet. Sushi lovers risk their lives for a portion of Fugu, as the fish is called in Japan. The family is closely related to the porcupinefish. Both are poor swimmers, which doesn't mean much in regard to their toxicity. The small Saddled Pufferfish, *Canthigaster valentini*, can be seen all around the islands of the Huvadhoo atoll, where they slowly swim in couples between coral heads. All family members are shy and rather difficult to approach. They feed on algae and a diverse array of invertebrates.

Lat: *Canthigaster bennetti*
Eng: Bennett's Pufferfish
Deu: Bennetts Krugfisch
Size: up to 9cm

Lat: *Canthigaster valentini*
Eng: Saddled Pufferfish
Deu: Sattel-Krugfisch
Size: up to 10cm

Lat: *Arothron nigropunctatus*
Eng: Black-spotted Pufferfish
Deu: Schwarzfleck-Kugelfisch
Size: up to 30cm

Porcupinefish

Lat: Diodontidae / Deu: Igelfische

Porcupinefish, as their name suggests, have spines all over their bodies. They are closely related to pufferfish and also blow themselves up by swallowing water, making them bigger and thus (they hope!) too big to be eaten. Many of them are also poisonous. Nevertheless, they are shy, hiding under corals and in little caves and cracks during the day. Porcupinefish feed on bivalves and snails. They have also been observed to feed on jellyfish.

Lat: *Diodon liturosus*
Eng: Blotched Porcupinefish
Deu: Masken-Igelfisch
Size: up to 50cm

Lat: *Diodon hystrix*
Eng: Black-spotted Porcupinefish
Deu: Gewöhnlicher Igelfisch
Size: up to 70cm

Sea turtles

Lat: Cheoniidae / Deu: Meeresschildkröten

Two of the most famous sea turtles of the world's oceans can be found in the Huvadhoo atoll, the Hawksbill and the Green Turtle. Both species are listed on the IUCN list of endangered species, mainly because their flesh and eggs are still regarded as delicacies in some countries. The Hawksbill Turtle is even regarded as being critically endangered, because it is also hunted for its shell which is used for making decorative objects and jewellery. Both species are also listed in Appendix 1 of CITES, which makes it illegal to import or export the animal or any products made from them. Honestly though, who would want to kill these beautiful and gentle animals anyway after having observed them swimming freely in the ocean?!

Especially in the Huvadhoo atoll, encounters with sea turtles during snorkelling and diving are almost guaranteed. As long as you remain calm and move slowly you can get really close to them. The main difference between the two species is the shape of their shells and the number of horny pairs of plates between the eyes. Hawksbill's shells have a saw-like rim and two pairs of horny plates between their eyes (see picture), whereas the Green Turtle has only a single pair and a rather smooth rimmed shell. Of course, the bill is a good discriminating character, too, as it is more round in the Green Turtle and more bird like in Hawksbills. This can often be difficult to see under water though. Another more important difference is their feeding modes. Green Turtles are exclusively herbivorous after the age of five years, whereas Hawksbills mostly feed on sponges and are therefore carnivores. They have also been observed to feed on jellyfish.

Lat: *Chelonia mydas*
Eng: Green Turtle
Deu: Suppenschildkröte
Size: up to 140cm

Lat: *Eretmochelys imbricata*
Eng: Hawksbill Turtle
Deu: Echte Karettschildkröte
Size: up to 90cm

Dolphins

Lat: Delphinidae / Deu: Delphine

Dolphins, or more specifically for this book, the Spinner Dolphin, *Stenella longirostris*, are unfortunately a rather seldom sight in the Huvadhoo atoll. If you do spot them you will most likely be able to observe huge groups of up to several hundred animals. These rather rare encounters are due to the size of the atoll and the dolphin's lifestyle and hunting practice in the open ocean. The chances to see them rise, but cannot be guaranteed, if you charter a boat for a private dolphin spotting excursion (see story: Partial solar eclipse, page 27). Start in the morning and ask your captain to take you to the outer reef. Trained eyes will spot them from afar by searching for Brown Noddies that flutter above the surface. The birds often indicate the presence of hunting tunas and these in turn often hunt in coalition with dolphins. Once you find them, some individuals will join the boat to ride the bow wave. The rest of the pack stays around the boat while showing off with spectacular spins. The actual reason behind these spins is still a mystery to science. Suggestions include such ideas as simple play, a hunting technique, inter-pack location communication, or a parasite ridding method. Whatever will finally be accepted as the true cause, it still remains a great spectacle.

Lat: *Stenella longirostris*
Eng: Spinner Dolphin
Deu: Spinner-Delphin
Size: up to 220cm

Ecological dive etiquette

Diving is one of the most rewarding sports in our modern, hectic world. Apart from the meditative rhythm of exhaled bubbles that whirl around your ears, the sea is silent and forces you to apply sign language. Imprisoned by limited means of communication, deaf by tons of surrounding water, numbed hands, no sense of smell and an endless taste of salt literally leave you alone with yourself and your last sense left, your vision. Accordingly, your thoughts circle around what you see and observe: an incredibly diverse world of colours, shapes and forms, a coral reef.

Being able to visit something as beautiful as a living coral reef means nothing less than to be extremely privileged. However, along with the privilege of visiting such a place comes the responsibility to protect and preserve it and if only out of respect for others who may subsequently follow us.

For these reasons there are some guidelines every responsible diver and snorkeller should adhere to. Divers often poetically summarize them as:

Touch nothing but water,
take nothing but pictures,
leave nothing but bubbles
and kill nothing but time!

From a practical point of view, the first part seems to be the easiest but is in fact the most dangerous and difficult to realise in coral reefs. For some it might come as a surprise, but in this respect it is not so much the hands of divers and snorkellers that cause damage but rather their sightless fins. Many people have long learned that it is wise not to touch that pretty pink sea anemone over there around the coral block, even though it looks so soft. Those blind fins at the rear end of the diver's body, however, are often forgotten. Protected in plastic and rubber, they crash into fragile Staghorn Corals and in a short moment of thoughtlessness, destroy decades of slow growth. The best way to avoid this kind of accidental destruction is perfect buoyancy. Unfortunately, even experienced and seasoned divers have often forgotten about this skill, especially after spending some time out of the water. In such a moment, a responsible diver subscribes to a refresher course with special attention to buoyancy training. Refreshed skills will also help divers in another very popular undertaking: photography. As we are not supposed to touch anything down in the deep, we must hover motionless in mid-water in order to take sharp pictures.

For snorkellers the situation is somewhat different. Just as with divers, the fins are the biggest threat to the coral community. However, there is a huge additional threat when it comes to snorkelling: convenience. Snorkellers often get tired and think it would be a great idea to take a rest over there on that big coral head, also known as a 'Porites' sofa. Now these big boulders might seem quite solid and in fact they can even destroy a ship's steel hull, but the truth is that the thin, living top layer is extremely sensitive to contact. The cells in this layer contain the stinging cells, nematocysts, designed to kill drifting plankton and they fire them at anything. Gigantic pink-blue striped boxer shorts and rubber boots are no exception.

Another common sight that makes the hearts and minds of marine biologists despair is when snorkellers walk over the reef to watch the edge beyond. In order to make the island's outer reef accessible to swimmers and snorkellers, many resorts dig out special channels through the reef to provide a safe passage. However, everybody is well advised to swim and not walk through these channels. Poisonous reef inhabitants like stone and scorpionfish can lurk anywhere and are easily stepped on. In case you should accidentally find yourself on top of the reef with only very limited space to move your fins, try not to use your hips or knees but restrict your fin movement to your ankles. This might feel somewhat boring and is certainly a very slow way to swim but it shows your commitment and care.

Yet another completely different implication of the 'no touch' rule even includes non-divers and non-snorkellers. The 'don't take' rule also refers to collectors of shells and other natural marine debris that is washed upon the beach. Unfortunately for the collectors, airport customs cannot differentiate between already dead collected shells and those that were taken alive out of their environment and sold in a shop. The same applies to shells collected under water. The alternatives are pictures taken with your watertight camera. Another tremendous advantage of these pictures is that the customs cannot fine you with humongous penalties or even lock you up in prison — though you can never be entirely sure about their intentions when you disembark from the plane looking healthily tanned, relaxed and happy about your holiday pictures. You might consider sending them a postcard before your next return!

Index

Dive sites – by type

Farus
17 – Dhevvamaagalaa Faru	44
18 – Funamaudoo Faru, Club Robinson Maldives	46
19 – Hagedhoo Faru	47
20 – Hirifushi Faru	48
21 – Gosi Faru	48
23 – Baulhageella Faru	50

Giris
6 – Coral City	34
11 – Haodi Galaa Giri	38
16 – Dheeva Giri	43
22 – Leon's Giri	49
24 – Kuda Giri	50
25 – Bodu Giri	51
33 – Mafzoo Giri	59

Thilas
2 – Fulangi Thila	27
4 – Mas Thila	30
5 – Wagaathu Galaa	31
7 – Hafsa Thila	35
9 – Meradhoo Thila	36
10 – Cabbage Thila	38
15 – Dheeva Thila	42
26 – Beyru Ha Thila	52
29 – Nilandhoo Thila	52
34 – Vadhoo Thila	59

Fushis
3 – Maafushi Beyru	29

Kandus
1 – Fulangi Kandu	26
8 – Meradhoo Kandu	36
12 – Kafena Kandu	39
13 – Rahadhoo Kandu	40
14 – Kaadedhdhoo Kandu	40
27 – Villingili Kandu	53
28 – Nilandhoo Kandu	54
30 – Vodamulaa Kandu	55
31 – Marehaa Kandu	58
32 – Kondey Kandu	58

Rudi in front of Vodamulaa Cave

Index

Icons

Rock lobster

Stingray

Grey Reef-shark

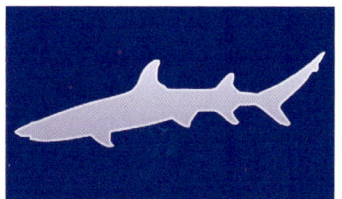
White-tip Reef-shark

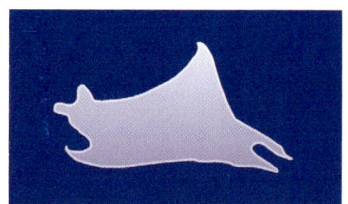
Mobula

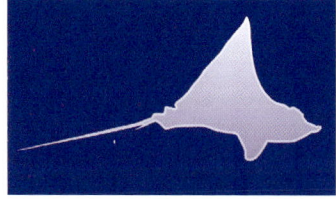
Eagle ray

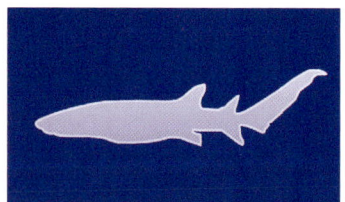
Nurse shark

Sea turtle

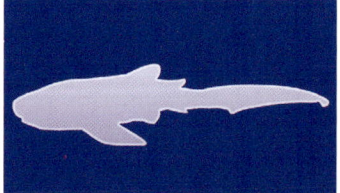
Zebra shark

Index

Butterflyfish

Batfish

Moray eel

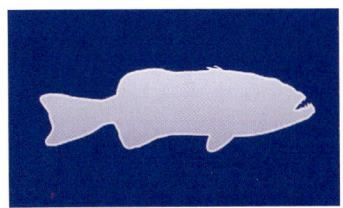
Grouper

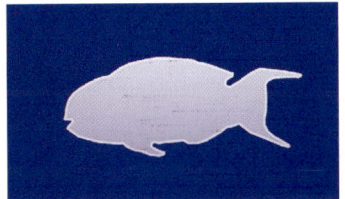
Parrotfish

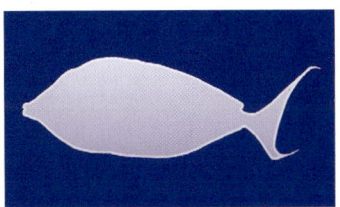
Surgeonfish

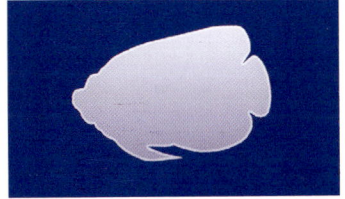
Angelfish

Sweetlip

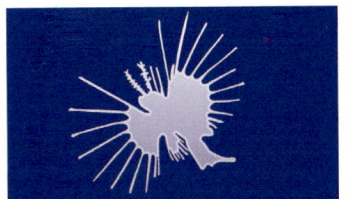
Lion and scorpionfish

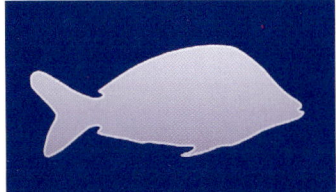
Snapper

205

Index

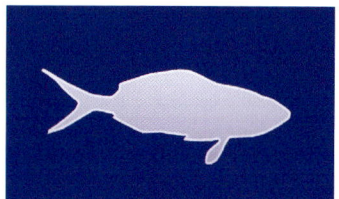
Fusilier

Wrasse

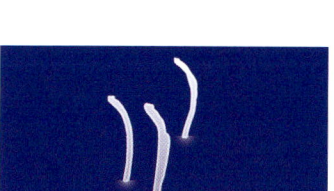
Garden eel

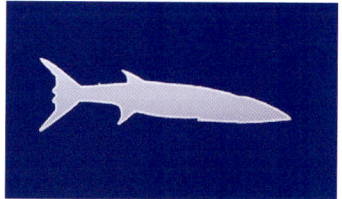
Barracuda

Jack and travelly

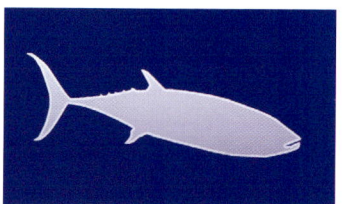
Tuna and mackerel

Common and scientific species & family names in Latin, English and German

A

68	Algae
165	*Abudefduf vaigiensis*
98	*Acanthaster planci*
183	Acanthuridae
184	*Acanthurus leucosternon*
184	*Acanthurus lineatus*
184	*Acanthurus mata*
183	*Acanthurus triostegus*
78	*Acropora cervicornis*
78	*Acropora hyacinthus*
77	*Acropora nasuta*
78	*Acropora palifera*
77	Acroporidae
117	Adlerrochen
134	*Aethaloperca rogaa*
117	*Aetobatus narinari*
174	Aggressiver Säbelzahn-Schleimfisch
97	Ägyptischer Seestern
72	Alcyoniidae
68	Algen
90	*Alpheus djiboutensis*
182	*Aluterus scriptus*
166	*Amblyglyphidodon leucogaster*
179	*Amblygobius hectori*
179	*Amblygobius semicinctus*
110	Ammenhaie
71	*Amphimedon* sp.
163	*Amphiprion clarkii*
162	*Amphiprion nigripes*
76	*Amplexidiscus fenestrafer*
102	Ananas Seewalze
159	Angelfish
74	*Annella mollis*
129	Antennenfeuerfisch
131	Anthiinae
132	*Anyperodon leocogrammicus*
138	*Apogon apogonoides*
137	*Apogon leptacanthus*
136	Apogonidae
159	*Apolemichthys trimaculatus*
136	*Archamia fucata*
193	*Arothron nigropunctatus*
137	Arrow-tooth Cardinalfish
105	*Ascidia glabra*
104	Ascidiacea
95	Asteroidea
127	Aulostomidae
127	*Aulostomus chinensis*
164	Azurblaue Demoiselle
164	Azure Damsel

B

190	*Balistapus undulatus*
190	Balistidae
191	*Balistoides conspicillum*
191	*Balistoides viridescens*
76	Balloon Corallimorph
91	Banded Boxer Shrimp
169	Banded Maori Wrasse
100	Banded Sea Urchin
140	Banded Trevally
186	Barracudas
186	Barrakudas
131	Basslets
180	Batfish
75	Beaded Anemone
70	Beeren-Schwamm
124	Belonidae
193	Bennett's Pufferfish
156	Bennetts Falterfisch
193	Bennetts Krugfisch
70	Berry Sponge
89	Big Blue Octopus
135	Bigeyes
74	Binsen Gorgonie
168	Bird Wrasse
85	Bivalves
85	Bivalvia
121	Black Cheek Moray
76	Black Coral Whip
153	Black Pyramid Butterflyfish
102	Black Sea Cucumber
143	Black Snapper
80	Black Sun Coral

207

Index

173	Black-dotted Sandperch	100	Burrowing Sea Urchin
133	Black-saddle Coral Grouper	160	Büschelbarsche
139	Black-spotted Pompano	153	Butterflyfish
194	Black-spotted Porcupinefish		
193	Black-spotted Pufferfish		
162	Blackfoot Anemonefish		
160	Blackside Hawkfish		**C**
81	Blasenkoralle		
191	Blasser Drückerfisch	145	*Caesio lunaris*
91	Blau Knie Einsiedler	144	*Caesio teres*
73	Blaue Koralle	144	*Caesio varilineata*
80	Blaue Poren-Koralle	145	*Caesio xanthonota*
71	Blauer Finger-Schwamm	144	Caesionidae
144	Blaugoldener Füsilier	74	Cane Gorgonia
185	Blauklingen-Nasendoktor	193	*Canthigaster bennetti*
159	Blaumasken-Kaiserfisch	193	*Canthigaster valentini*
166	Blaupunkt-Riffbarsch	139	Carangidae
178	Blaupunkt-Schläfergrundel	140	*Carangoides ferdau*
142	Blaustreifen Schnapper	140	*Caranx melampygus*
184	Blaustreifen-Doktorfisch	113	Carcharhinidae
174	Blaustreifen-Säbelzahn-Schleimfisch	113	*Carcharhinus amblyrhynchos*
100	Bleistift-Diademseeigel	136	Cardinalfish
175	*Blenniella chrysospilos*	81	Caryophylliidae
174	Blennies	94	*Cenometra bella*
174	Blenniidae	133	*Cephalopholis argus*
115	Blotched Fantail Ray	133	*Cephalopholis miniata*
194	Blotched Porcupinefish	75	*Cerianthus* sp.
73	Blue Coral	171	*Cetoscarus bicolor*
80	Blue Pore Coral	156	*Chaetodon bennetti*
191	Blue Triggerfish	154	*Chaetodon falcula*
140	Blue-fin Jack	154	*Chaetodon kleinii*
71	Blue-finger Sponge	154	*Chaetodon lunula*
163	Blue-green Puller	155	*Chaetodon madagaskariensis*
105	Blue-spot Sea Squirt	158	*Chaetodon meyeri*
128	Blue-spotted Cornetfish	155	*Chaetodon ornatissimus*
167	Blue-streak Cleaner Wrasse	158	*Chaetodon oxycephalus*
142	Blue-striped Snapper	155	*Chaetodon triangulum*
164	Blue-yellow Damsel	155	*Chaetodon trifasciatus*
125	Blutfleck-Husar	157	*Chaetodon xanthocephalus*
175	Blutstropfen-Felshüpfer	156	*Chaetodon zanzibariensis*
170	*Bodianus axillaris*	153	Chaetodontidae
101	*Bohadschia graeffei*	85	*Chama lazerus*
100	Bohrseeigel	158	*Cheatodon auriga*
191	Boomerang Triggerfish	168	Checkerboard Wrasse
188	Bothidae	169	*Cheilinus fasciatus*
188	*Bothus pantherinus*	170	*Cheilinus trilobatus*
189	Boxfish	170	*Cheilinus undulatus*
80	Brain Coral	137	*Cheilodipterus artus*
121	Breedens Muräne	137	*Cheilodipterus macrodon*
178	*Brianinops* sp.	195	*Chelonia mydas*
74	Broccoli Coral	195	Cheoniidae
74	Brokkoli Koralle	181	Chin-strap Rabbitfish
154	Brown Butterflyfish	74	*Chironephthya* sp.
143	Buckel-Schnapper	110	Chondrichthys
172	Bullethead Parrotfish	103	Chordata

103	Chordates	197	Delphinidae
103	Chordatiere	70	Demospongiae
97	*Choriaster granulatus*	73	*Dendronephthya* sp. 1
163	*Chromis atripectoralis*	74	*Dendronephthya* sp. 2
164	*Chromis ternatensis*	80	*Dendrophyllia gracilis*
165	*Chrysiptera brownriggii*	80,81	Dendrophylliidae
166	*Chrysiptera unimaculata*	125	Diadem-Husar
161	*Cirrhitichthys oxycephalus*	104	*Didemnum molle*
160	Cirrhitidae	194	*Diodon hystrix*
163	Clark's Anemonefish	194	*Diodon liturosus*
163	Clarks Anemonenfisch	194	Diodontidae
105	*Clavelina moluccensis*	130	*Diploprion bifasciatum*
191	Clown Triggerfish	90	Djibouti Knallkrebs
93	*Colobometra perspinosa*	90	Djibouti Snapping Shrimp
78	Column Staghorn Coral	187	Dogtooth Tuna
129	Common Lionfish	193	Doktorfische
80	Common Mushroom Coral	197	Dolphins
88	Common Spider Shell	151	Doppelband-Meerbarbe
87	Common Turban shell	143	Doppelfleck-Schnapper
183	Convict Surgeonfish	98	Dornenkrone
85	Coral Clam	138	Dornenkronen-Kardinalbarsch
170	Coral Hogfish	151	Double-bar Goatfish
71	Coral-eating Sponge	154	Double-saddle Butterflyfish
88	*Coriacella hibyae*	129	Drachenköpfe
128	Cornetfish	76	Drahtkoralle
126	*Corythoichtys haematopterus*	163	Dreibinden-Preussenfisch
116	Cowtail Stingray	176	Dreiflossen-Schleimfische
175	Crested Sabretooth Blenny	159	Dreipunkt-Rauchkaiserfisch
93	Crinoidea	170	Dreizack-Prachtlippfisch
124	Crocodile Needlefish	190	Drückerfische
86	Crocus Giant Clam	165	Dunkelblaue Gelbschwanz-Demoiselle
177	Crocus Shrimp Goby	132	Dunkelflossen-Forellenbarsch
125	Crown Squirrelfish		
138	Crown-of-thorns Cardinalfish		
98	Crown-of-thorns Sea Star	**E**	
90	Crustacea		
90	Crustaceans	117	Eagle Rays
184	*Ctenochtaetus striatus*	141	Echeneidae
184	*Ctenochtaetus strigosus*	141	*Echeneis naucrates*
177	*Ctenogobiops crocineus*	92	Echinodermata
96	*Culcita schmedeliana*	92	Echinoderms
79	Cylinder Coral	99	Echinoidea
88	*Cypraea tigris*	100	*Echinometra mathaei*
		100	*Echinostrephus molaris*
D		100	*Echinothrix calamaris*
		196	Echte Karettschildkröte
162	Damselfish	156	Eclipse Butterflyfish
91	*Dardanus lagopodes*	175	*Ecsenius bicolor*
91	*Dardanus megistos*	175	*Ecsenius lineatus*
145	Dark-banded Fusilier	175	*Ecsenius minutus*
163	*Dascyllus aruanus*	102	Edible Sea Cucumber
163	*Dascyllus carneaus*	97	Egyptian Sea Star
151	Dash-and-dot Goatfish	123	Eidechsenfische
115	Dasyatididae	166	Einfleck-Demoiselle
197	Delphine		

Index

86	Eingewachsene Riesenmuschel
140	*Elagatis bipinnulata*
88	Elegant Phyllidia
88	Elegante Warzenschnecke
74	*Ellisella* sp.
74	Ellisellidae
169	Emperor Angelfish
149	Emperors
76	Encrusting Anemone
180	Ephippidae
132	Epinephelinae
134	*Epinephelus caeruleopunctatus*
134	*Epinephelus spilotoceps*
196	*Eretmochelys imbricata*
102	Essbare Seegurke

F

137	Fadenflossen-Kardinalbarsch
130	Fahnenbarsche
158	Falscher Riesenfalter
153	Falterfische
157	Fantom-Wimpelfisch
93	Feather stars
116	Federschwanz-Stechrochen
192	Feilenfische
132	Fenster-Zackenbarsch
192	Filefish
184	Fine-lined Bristletooth
128	*Fistularia commersonii*
128	Fistulariidae
79	Flame Coral
79	Flammen-Koralle
69	Flaschenbürstenalge
180	Fledermausfische
128	Flötenfisch
128	Flötenfische
88	Flügelschnecke
86	Fluted Giant Clam
155	*Forcipiger flavissimus*
160	Forsters Büschelbarsch
134	Foursaddle Grouper
129	Fransen-Drachenkopf
96	*Fromia indica*
95	*Fromia mileporella*
96	*Fromia nodosa*
80	*Fungia fungites*
80	Fungiidae
178	*Fusigobius* sp.
144	Füsiliere
144	Fusiliers

G

139	Gabelschwanz-Makrele
98	Galathea Sea Star
98	Galatheas Seestern
122	Garden Eel
122	Garden eels
87	Gastropoda
91	Gebänderte Scherengarnele
117	Gefleckter Adlerrochen
161	Gefleckter Korallenwächter
97	Gekörnter Kissenstern
189	Gelbbrauner-Kofferfisch
73	Gelbe Bäumchen-Weichkoralle
81	Gelbe Salatkoralle
74	Gelbhäutige Weichkoralle
149	Gelbflossen-Straßenkehrer
185	Gelbklingen-Nasendoktor
158	Gelbkopf-Falterfisch
142	Gelbkopf-Schnapper
145	Gelbrücken-Füsilier
151	Gelbsattel-Meerbarbe
190	Gelbschwanz-Drücker
131	Gelbschwanz-Fahnenbarsch
146	Gerreidae
146	*Gerres acinaces*
91	Gestreifte Languste
141	Gestreifter Schiffshalter
78	Geweihkoralle
87	Gewöhnliche Turbanschnecke
129	Gewöhnlicher Feuerfisch
194	Gewöhnlicher Igelfisch
167	Gewöhnlicher Putzerlippfisch
120	Giant Moray
190	Giant Triggerfish
88	Gift-Warzenschnecke
110	Ginglymostomatidae
183	Gitter-Doktorfisch
75	Glasperlen-Anemone
86	Glatte Riesenmuschel
105	Glatte Seescheide
149	*Gnathodentex aureolineatus*
150	Goatfish
177	Gobies
177	Gobiidae
178	*Gobiodon citrinus*
184	Gold-ring Bristletooth
149	Gold-spot Emperor
138	Goldbauch-Kardinalbarsch
181	Goldfleck-Kaninchenfisch
149	Goldfleck-Straßenkehrer
184	Goldring-Borstenzahndoktor
177	Goldstreifen-Grundel
149	Goldstreifen-Straßenkehrer
97	*Gomophia egyptiaca*

168	*Gomphosus caeruleus*	152	Heller Ruderbarsch
80	Graceful Coral	169	*Hemigymnus melapterus*
132	*Gracila albomarginata*	153	*Hemitaurichthys zoster*
101	Graeffe's Sea Cucumber	80	Hemprichi's Brain Coral
101	Graeffes Seewalze	80	Hemprichis Hirnkoralle
130	Grammistini	157	*Heniochus diphreutes*
97	Granulated Sea Star	157	*Heniochus pleurotaenia*
113	Grauer Riffhai	75	*Heteractis aurora*
80	Grazile Kelchkoralle	76	*Heteractis magnifica*
186	Great Barracuda	99	*Heterocentrotus mammillatus*
195	Green Turtle	122	*Heteroconger hassi*
172	Green-face Parrotfish	122	Heterocongridae
113	Grey Reef-shark	75	Hexacorallia
99	Griffel-Seeigel	88	Hiby's Lamellarid
135	Großaugenbarsche	94	*Himerometra robustipinna*
76	Grosses Elefantenohr	145	Himmelblauer Füsilier
79	Grosse Porenkoralle	125	Holocentridae
186	Großer Barrakuda	102	*Holothuria atra*
129	Großer Schaukelfisch	102	*Holothuria edulis*
149	Großkopf-Schnapper	101	Holothurians
150	Großschulen-Meerbarbe	86	Honeycomb Oyster
132	Groupers	86	Honigwabenauster
177	Grundeln	124	Hornhechte
104	Grüne Riffseescheide	70	Hornkieselschwämme
97	Guilding's Sea Star	94	Hübscher Haarstern
97	Guildings Seestern	163	Humbug Damsel
187	*Gymnosarda unicolor*	79	Hump Coral
121	*Gymnothorax breedeni*	143	Humpback Snapper
120	*Gymnothorax javanicus*	187	Hundezahn-Thunfisch
		125	Husarenfische
		78	Hyazinthen-Tischkoralle
		86	*Hyotissa hyotis*

H

93	Haarsterne
147	Haemulidae
91	Hairy Red Hermit Crab
191	Halbmond-Drückerfisch
169	Half-and-half Wrasse
191	Half-moon Triggerfish
182	Halfterfisch
168	*Halichoeres hortulanus*
71	*Haliclona nematifera*
175	Halsband-Wippschwimmer
77	Hard coral
169	Hardwickes Junker
147	Harlekin Süßlippe
147	Harlequin Sweetlip
160	Hawkfish
196	Hawksbill Turtle
179	Hector Grundel
179	Hector's Reef-goby
176	*Helcogramma maldivensis*
73	*Heliopora coerulea*
73	Helioporidae

I

194	Igelfische
116	Igelrochen
125	Immaculate Soldierfish
159	Imperator-Kaiserfisch
174	Imposter Blenny
163	Indian Damsel
163	Indian Humbug
96	Indian Sea Star
163	Indische Demoiselle
155	Indischer Baroness-Falterfisch
172	Indischer Buckelkopf
96	Indischer Kissen-Seestern
163	Indischer Preussenfisch
96	Indischer Seestern
165	Indopazifik-Sergeant
110	Indopazifischer Ammenhai
135	Indopazifischer Großaugenbarsch
85	Irisierende Kammmuschel

Index

J

139	Jacks and trevally
166	Jewel Damsel
131	Juwelen-Fahnenbarsch
133	Juwelen-Zackenbarsch

K

159	Kaiserfische
181	Kaninchenfische
136	Kardinalsfische
154	Keilfleck-Falterfisch
146	Kleinbeschuppter Mojarra
154	Kleins Falterfisch
96	Knotiger Seestern
189	Kofferfische
98	Kometenstern
71	Korallenfressender Schwamm
160	Korallenwächter
90	Krebse
124	Krokodil-Hornhecht
76	Krustenbildende Anemone
193	Kugelfische
172	Kugelkopf-Papageifisch
152	Kyphosidae
152	*Kyphosus cinerascens*

L

167	Labridae
168	*Labroides bicolor*
167	*Labroides dimidiatus*
88	*Lambis lambis*
184	Langnasendoktor
184	Längsstreifen-Doktorfisch
175	Längsstreifen-Wippschwimmer
129	Leaf fish
188	Lefteye Flounder
188	Leopard Flounder
191	Leoparden-Drückerfisch
149	Lethrinidae
149	*Lethrinus erythracanthus*
149	*Lethrinus obsoletus*
126	Liegende Seenadel
97	*Linckia guldingi*
98	*Linckia multifora*
175	Lined Combtooth Blenny
184	Lined Surgeonfish
188	Linksaugen-Flunder
129	Lion- and scorpionfish
167	Lippfische
74	*Litophyton arboreum*
175	Little Combtooth Blenny
123	Lizardfish
80	*Lobophyllia hemprichii*
155	Long-nose Butterflyfish
192	Long-nose Filefish
137	Long-spine Cardinalfish
132	Lunar-tailed Grouper
142	Lutjanidae
143	*Lutjanus biguttatus*
143	*Lutjanus bohar*
143	*Lutjanus gibbus*
142	*Lutjanus kasmira*

M

187	Mackerels
142	*Macolor macularis*
143	*Macolor niger*
155	Madagascar Butterflyfish
155	Madagaskar-Falterfisch
74	Magenta Bäumchen-Weichkoralle
74	Magenta Soft Coral
76	Magnificent Sea Anemone
187	Makrelen
176	Maldives Triplefin
162	Malediven Anemonenfisch
174	Malediven-Säbelzahn-Schleimfisch
88	Malediven-Schwammschnecke
176	Maledivischer Dreiflossen-Schleimfisch
119	*Manta birostris*
119	Manta Ray
194	Masken-Igelfisch
171	Masken-Papageifisch
100	Mathae's Sea Urchin
150	Meerbarben
195	Meeresschildkröten
69	Meertraube
174	*Meiacanthus smithi*
158	Meyer's Butterflyfish
158	Meyers Falterfisch
142	Midnight Snapper
118	*Mobula eregoodootenkee*
146	Mojarras
84	Mollusca
84	Molluscs
105	Molukken-Keulenseescheide
192	Monacanthidae
154	Mondsichel-Falterfisch
132	Mondsichel-Juwelenbarsch
161	Monokel-Büschelbarsch
145	Moon Fusilier

135	Moontail Bullseye		149	Orange-striped Emperor
182	Moorish Idol		136	Orangelined Cardinalfish
120	Moray eels		178	Orangepunkt-Grundel
150	Mullidae		155	Orangestreifen-Falterfisch
150	*Mulloides vanicolensis*		136	Orangestreifen-Kardinalbarsch
98	Multi-pore Sea Star		147	Orient-Süßlippe
120	*Muraenidae*		147	Oriental Sweetlip
120	Muränen		155	Ornate Butterflyfish
85	Muscheln		120	Osteichthyes
73	Mushroom Leather Coral		189	*Ostracion cubicus*
80	Mussidae		189	Ostrociidae
117	Myliobatidae		192	*Oxymonacanthus longirostris*
125	*Myripristis vittata*			

N

P

			91	Painted Rock Lobster
170	Napoleon		184	Pale Surgeonfish
98	*Nardoa galatheae*		192	Palettenstachler
77	Nasen-Koralle		188	Pantherbutt
184	*Naso brevirostris*		91	*Panulirus versicolor*
185	*Naso hexacanthus*		171	Papageifische
185	*Naso lituratus*		129	Paper Scorpionfish
110	*Nebrius ferrugineus*		161	*Paracirrhites arcatus*
86	Necklace Giant Clam		160	*Paracirrhites forsteri*
124	Needlefish		173	*Parapercis hexophthalama*
179	*Nemateleotris magnifica*		173	*Parapercis millipunctata*
148	Nemipteridae		70	*Paratetilla bacca*
145	Neon-Füsilier		171	Parrotfish
125	*Neoniphon sammara*		151	*Parupeneus barberinus*
73	Nephthidae		151	*Parupeneus bifasciatus*
74	Nidaliidae		151	*Parupeneus cyclostomus*
96	Noduled Sea Star		116	*Pastinachus sephen*
77	Nosey Coral		133	Peacock Rock Cod
110	Nurse sharks		85	*Pedum spondyloidum*
			85	Penguin Wing Oyster
			85	Perlmuschel
			175	*Petroscirtes mitratus*
			164	Pfauen-Demoiselle
			159	Pfauen-Kaiserfisch

O

73	Octocorallia		133	Pfauen-Zackenbarsch
89	Octopodidae		140	Pferdemakrele
89	*Octopus cyanea*		157	Phantom Bannerfish
89	Octopuses		165	Philippine Damsel
191	*Odonus niger*		88	*Phyllidia elegans*
122	Ohrfleck-Röhrenaal		88	*Phyllidia varicosa*
89	Oktopusse		88	*Phyllidiella rosans*
166	One-spot Damsel		157	Pig-face Butterflyfish
131	Orange Basslet		80	Pilz-Koralle
73	Orange Soft Coral		73	Pilz-Lederkoralle
185	Orange-spine Unicornfish		102	Pineapple Sea Cucumber
175	Orange-spotted Blenny		173	Pinguipedidae
149	Orange-spotted Emperor		155	Pinstriped Butterflyfish
178	Orange-spotted Sand-goby		126	Pipefish

Index

174	*Plagiotremus phenax*
174	*Plagiotremus rhinorhynchos*
138	Plain Cardinalfish
180	*Platax orbicularis*
78	Plate Coral
147	*Plectorhinchus chaetodonoides*
147	*Plectorhinchus vittatus*
166	*Plectroglyphidodon lacrymatus*
132	*Plectropomus areolatus*
133	*Plectropomus laevis*
81	*Plerogyra sinuosa*
69	Pom Pom Algae
159	Pomacanthidae
159	*Pomacanthus imperator*
159	*Pomacanthus xanthometopon*
162	Pomacentridae
164	*Pomacentrus caeruleus*
163	*Pomacentrus indicus*
164	*Pomacentrus pavo*
165	*Pomacentrus philippinus*
116	Porcupine Ray
194	Porcupinefish
70	Porifera
79	*Porites lobata*
79	*Porites cylindrica*
79	*Porites rus*
80	*Porites* sp.
79,80	Poritidae
184	Powder-blue Surgeonfish
76	Prachtanemone
179	Pracht-Schwertgrundel
94	Pretty Feather Star
135	Priacanthidae
135	*Priacanthus hamrur*
131	*Pseudanthias evansi*
131	*Pseudanthias squamipinnis*
85	*Pteria penguin*
145	*Pterocaesio tile*
129	*Pterois antennata*
129	*Pterois volitans*
193	Pufferfish
146	Pursemouths
118	Pygmy Devil Ray
159	*Pygoplites diacanthus*

Q

140	Querstreifen-Makrele

R

181	Rabbitfish
154	Racoon Butterflyfish
140	Rainbow Runner
143	Red Bass
179	Red Fire-goby
91	Red Hermit Crab
134	Red-flushed Grouper
68	Redalgae
126	Reef-top Pipefish
140	Regenbogen-Renner
141	Remoras
113	Requiem Haie
113	Requiem sharks
138	*Rhabdamia cypselura*
112	Rhincodontidae
68	*Rhodophyta* sp.
102	Riesen Seewalze
191	Riesen-Drückerfisch
74	Riesenfächer
125	Riesenhusar
119	Riesenmanta
120	Riesenmuräne
123	Riff-Eidechsenfisch
162	Riffbarsche
100	Riffdachseeigel
112	*Rincodon typus*
161	Ring-eye Hawkfish
155	Rippen-Falterfisch
94	Robust Feather Star
94	Robuster Haarstern
122	Röhrenaale
155	Röhrenmaul-Pinzettfisch
88	Rosa Warzenschnecke
88	Rose Phyllidiella
68	Rotalge
169	Rotbrust-Prachtlippfisch
89	Roter Krake
134	Rotmaul-Zackenbarsch
191	Rotzahn-Drückerfisch
85	Rough Cockle
180	Rounded Batfish
159	Royal Angelfish
102	Royal Sea Cucumber
152	Rudderfish
152	Ruderbarshe
188	Rundkopf-Fledermausfisch

S

125	Sabre Squirrelfish	195	Sea turtles
193	Saddled Pufferfish	99	Sea urchins
130	Sägebarsche	75	Sechsstrahlige Blumentiere
69	Sailor's Eyeball Algae	101	Seegurken
173	Sandbarsche	99	Seeigel
173	Sandperch	93	Seelilien
156	Sansibar-Falterfisch	126	Seenadeln
73	*Sarcophyton* sp.	178	Seepeitschen Grundel
125	*Sargocentron diadema*	104	Seescheiden
125	*Sargocentron spiniferum*	95	Seesterne
133	Sattel-Forellenbarsch	101	Seewalzen
193	Sattel-Krugfisch	175	Segelflossen-Säbelzahn-Schleimfisch
78	Säulen-Geweihkoralle	130	Seifenbarsche
171	Scaridae	165	Sergeant Mayor
172	*Scarus prasiognathus*	130	Serranidae
172	*Scarus sordidus*	172	Sheephead Parrotfish
172	*Scarus strongylocephalus*	181	Siganidae
168	Schachbrett-Junker	181	*Siganus guttatus*
148	Schärpen-Scheinschnapper	181	*Siganus puelloides*
102	Scheckige Seewalze	181	*Siganus stellatus*
148	Scheinschnapper	70	Silicious Sponges
141	Schiffshalter	172	Singapur-Papageifisch
174	Schleimfische	81	Sinuose Coral
96	Schmedelian Pincushion Sea Star	138	*Siphamia fuscolineata*
142	Schnapper	169	Six-bar Wrasse
87	Schnecken	178	Six-spot Sleeper-goby
134	Schneeflocken-Zackenbarsch	99	Slate-pencil Sea Urchin
157	Schooling Bannerfish	185	Sleek Unicornfish
192	Schrift-Feilenfisch	141	Slender Suckerfish
86	Schuppige Riesenmuschel	146	Small-scale Pursemouth
138	Schwalbenschwanz-Kardinalbarsch	134	Small-spotted Grouper
173	Schwanzfleck-Sandbarsch	129	Smallscale Scorpionfish
157	Schwarm-Wimpelfisch	174	Smith's Venomous Blenny
163	Schwarzachsel-Schwalbenschwänzchen	105	Smooth Ascidia
184	Schwarzdorn-Doktorfisch	74	Smooth Sea Fan
85	Schwarze Flügelmuschel	142	Snapper
80	Schwarze Kelchkoralle	152	Snubnose Rudderfish
102	Schwarze Seegurke	130	Soapfish
153	Schwarzer Pyramiden-Falterfisch	73	Soft coral
193	Schwarzfleck-Kugelfisch	104	Soft Didemnum
115	Schwarzpunktrochen	125	Soldatenfische
143	Schwarzweiß-Schnapper	125	Soldierfish
77	Scleractinia	173	Speckled Sandperch
148	*Scolopsis bilineata*	71	*Spheciospongia cf. vagabunda*
187	Scombridae	186	*Sphyraena barracuda*
129	Scorpaenidae	186	Sphyraenidae
129	*Scorpaenopsis oxycephala*	197	Spinner Dolphin
192	Scrawled Filefish	197	Spinner-Delphin
130	Sea bass	93	Spinose Feather Star
101	Sea cucumbers	132	Spitzkopf-Zackenbarsch
93	Sea lilies	86	*Spondylus varius*
95	Sea stars	70	Sponges
104	Sea squirts	129	Spotfin Lionfish
		125	Spotfin Squirrelfish
		117	Spotted Eagle Ray

Index

161	Spotted Hawkfish
102	Spotted Sea Cucumber
184	Spotted Unicornfish
132	Squaretail Coral Grouper
125	Squirrelfish
181	Sri Lankan Rabbitfish
86	Stachelauster
92	Stachelhäuter
139	Stachelmakrelen
80	Stachlige Faltenkoralle
93	Stachliger Haarstern
78	Staghorn Coral
181	Starry Rabbitfish
115	Stechrochen
111	*Stegostoma fasciatum*
111	Stegostomatidae
77	Steinkorallen
197	*Stenella longirostris*
91	*Stenopus hispidus*
152	Steuerbarsche
76	*Stichopathes* sp.
102	*Stichopus variegatus*
115	Stingrays
151	Strichpunkt-Meerbarbe
190	Striped Triggerfish
74	Subergorgiidae
191	*Sufflamen bursa*
191	*Sufflamen chrysopterus*
195	Suppenschildkröte
165	Surge Damsel
183	Surgeonfish
147	Süßlippen
164	Swallow-tail Puller
138	Swallowtail Cardinalfish
147	Sweetlips
80	*Symphyllia agaricia*
102	*Synapta maculata*
126	Syngnathidae
123	Synodontidae
123	*Synodus variegatus*

T

129	*Taenianotus triacanthus*
115	*Taeniura meyeni*
95	Tausend Poren Seestern
110	Tawny Nurse Shark
87	*Tectus niloticus*
164	Ternate-Schwalbenschwanz
129	Tesseled Scorpionfish
193	Tetraodontidae
169	*Thalassoma hardwicke*
102	*Thelenota ananas*
102	*Thelenota anax*
144	Thin-lined Fusilier
95	Thousand Pores Sea Star
148	Threadfin Bream
158	Threadfin Butterflyfish
159	Threespot Angelfish
187	Thunfische
137	Tiger Cardinalfish
88	Tiger Cowry
137	Tiger-Kardinalbarsch
88	Tiger-Kaurie
191	Titan Triggerfish
139	*Trachinotus baillonii*
181	Traueraugen-Kaninchenfisch
114	*Triaenodon obesus*
155	Triangular Butterflyfish
86	*Tridacna crocea*
86	*Tridacna derasa*
86	*Tridacna squamosa*
190	Triggerfish
170	Triple-tail Maori Wrasse
176	Triplefins
176	Tripterygiidae
127	Trompetenfisch
127	Trumpetfish
75	Tube Anemone
80	*Tubastraea micrantha*
174	Tube-worm Blenny
187	Tuna
181	Tüpfel-Kaninchenfisch
81	*Turbinaria reniformis*
168	Two-colour Cleaner Wrasse
175	Two-colour Combtooth Blenny
171	Two-colour Parrotfish
148	Two-lined Monocle Bream
143	Two-spot Snapper
69	*Tydemania expeditionis*
124	*Tylosurus crocodilus*

U

87	Univalves
116	*Urogymnus asperrimus*

V

71	Vagabond Sponge
71	Vagabunden Schwamm
178	*Valenciennea sexguttata*
69	*Valonia ventricosa*
86	Variable Thorny Oyster

88	Varicose Phyllidia			
123	Variegated Lizardfish			
102	Varigated Sea Cucumber		132	Zackenbarsche
132	*Variola louti*		182	Zanclidae
133	Vermillion Rock Cod		76	*Zanthus* sp.
173	Vielpunkt-Sandbarsch		156	Zanzibar Butterflyfish
144	Vielstreifen-Füsilier		111	Zebra shark
134	Vierfleck-Wabenbarsch		111	Zebrahai
168	Vogel-Lippfisch		178	Zitronengrundel

Z

132	Zackenbarsche
182	Zanclidae
76	*Zanthus* sp.
156	Zanzibar Butterflyfish
111	Zebra shark
111	Zebrahai
178	Zitronengrundel
168	Zweifarb-Putzerlippfisch
169	Zweifarben-Bannerlippfisch
175	Zweifarben-Wippschwimmer
143	Zweifleck-Schnapper
170	Zweifleck-Schweinslippfisch
130	Zweistreifen-Seifenbarsch
118	Zwerg-Teufelsrochen
79	Zylinder-Koralle
75	Zylinderrose

W

112	Walhai
73	Weichkorallen
84	Weichtiere
179	Weißband-Schläfergrundel
166	Weißbauch-Riffbarsch
184	Weißkehl-Doktorfisch
91	Weißpunkt-Einsiedler
114	Weissspitzen-Riffhai
125	Weißspitzen-Soldatenfisch
165	Wellen-Demoiselle
112	Whale Shark
178	Whip Goby
179	White-barred Reef-goby
166	White-breasted Sergeant
132	White-lined Grouper
132	White-square Grouper
114	White-tip Reef-shark
137	Wolfskardinalbarsch
167	Wrasses
102	Wurmseegurke

Y

189	Yellow Boxfish
178	Yellow Coral-goby
74	Yellow Naked Soft Coral
130	Yellow Soapfish
81	Yellow Stony Coral
144	Yellow-and-blueback Fusilier
145	Yellow-back Fusilier
158	Yellow-head Butterflyfish
151	Yellow-saddle Goatfish
150	Yellow-stripe Goatfish
131	Yellow-tail Basslet
159	Yellowface Angelfish

About the author

Alexander von Mende is a marine biologist and travelling diver who studied marine biology in Germany, the Arctic and Peru. He has worked in the diving industry in Greece and the Maldives. Puts his pen where his thoughts are. Knows too much to close his eyes and has experienced too little to simply shut up. This is his first book.

Acknowledgements

This moment, as I write these lines, is a truly great one for me. First, because it means that the book is about to be published and secondly, because it simply feels amazing. On the other hand you start realising how many people actually helped with such a seemingly small task as producing the book. And this is where the real problem starts: Whom do I have to thank first?

Many thanks go out to all the people at Silver Sands Pvt. Ltd. in the Maldives, especially Rüdiger Palm, without whom I wouldn't even have made it to Huvadhoo. Also, I wish to thank my dear colleagues: Julia Jagoditsch, who edited the pictures and drew the map of Huvadhoo, Saif Deen who drew all the divesite maps, shared his knowledge and is undoubtedly the best dive-master I know, and of course Christian Gratz for great dives and good moments with decompression beers.

Furthermore, I must not forget to thank Paul Carthew and Nicola and Hugh Loxdale for countless hours of proof reading and tons of valuable hints on the manuscript.

And last but certainly not least, I express my love to my girlfriend Emeline Gaufreteau. It was her patience and confidence in me that enabled me to complete this work. My deepest gratitude also goes to her family who supported me in difficult times and her brother, Vincent 'Tibeon' Gaufreteau for the fantastic layout and patience in designing the book.

Photography references

All pictures copyright by Alexander von Mende, except:

Page 15, Ibrahim Nasir portrait: unknown author

Pages 110-112, 119 & 186: Silver Sands Pvt. Ldt.

Page 159 *Pomacanthus imperator*: Julia Jagoditsch

Page 218, Picture of the author: Emeline Gaufreteau

A Selection of other natural history books by Brambleby Books

ISBN 9780954334734
Bird Words – Poetic images of wild birds
Hugh D. Loxdale
This poetry book reminds us that wild birds continue to inspire and delight in a host of different ways.

ISBN 9780954334796
Arrivals and Rivals – A duel for the winning bird
Adrian Riley
A rich and gripping personal tale about competitive birdwatching, full of humour and humanity.

ISBN 9780954334789
UK500: Birding in the fast lane
James Hanlon
A huge tribute to one man's determination to see the most bird species in the UK before he turned 30.

ISBN 9780954334772
Feathers and Eggshells – A bird journal of a young London girl
Natalie Lawrence
A delightful journal by a young London girl, describing the wild birds of Hampstead Heath using drawings, photographs, prose and poetry.

ISBN 9780955392801
British and Irish Butterflies
Adrian Riley
The complete field, identification and site guide to the species, subspecies and forms in full colour.

ISBN 9780954334741
The Flora of Berkshire
Michael J. Crawley
A comprehensive and timely Flora by one of Britain's leading plant ecologists.

ISBN 9780955392849
The Wild Flowers of the Isle of Purbeck
Edward Pratt
An essential companion for walks on the Isle of Purbeck.

ISBN 9780955392832
Garden Photo Shoot – A Photographer's Year-book of Garden Wildlife
John Thurlbourn
A charming illustrated garden wildlife book.

ISBN 9780955392818
What's in your Garden – A book for young explorers
Colin Spedding
This book is all about exploring and discovery for children, age 7-11 years.

ISBN 9780955392856
Winging it – Birding for low-flyers
Andrew Fallan
Enjoyment and adventures of birdwatching from child- to adulthood.

ISBN 9780955392870
Never a dull moment – A naturalist's view of British wildlife
Ross Gardner
Brilliant philosophical musings about the diverse wildlife of Britain

ISBN 9781908241030
Backpacker Naturalist – Wild times down under
James Hanlon
A memorable travelogue of a young naturalist seeking adventure in New Zealand and Australia.

ISBN 9781908241054
The Call of the Kokako – Poems from far-flung places
Anthony Boniface
A collection of philosophical poems, inspired by travelling the world.

www.bramblebybooks.co.uk